HOLY AMBITION

"Integrating faith and work is something I have been passionate about for many years. I loved diving into Taryn DeLong and Elise Crawford Gallagher's new book, *Holy Ambition*, to get their take on this important topic and gain a better understanding of the unique gifts Catholic women bring to the workplace. This book is an excellent resource not only for Catholic women in the workplace seeking to more fully integrate their faith and work but also for men to better understand the important experiences, motivations, and insights of Catholic female professionals. I will absolutely recommend and gift this book to women and men in my network who will benefit from the wisdom it contains."

Randy Hain
Author and president of Serviam Partners

"As his daughters, we are made to participate in our heavenly Father's creative and redemptive work. Yet the delicate dance of caring, providing, and becoming—at work and home—can be both exquisitely joyful and painful. When a woman wonders 'How do I do this?,' DeLong and Gallagher compassionately remind her what our enemy wants us to forget: the keys to true joy and fruitful work are embracing our God-given nature and surrendering to his even more magnificent dreams for us."

Claire Dwyer
Author and cofounder of Write These Words

"DeLong and Gallagher have offered a powerful resource for women who understand their work in the world as a vocation and yearn for it to be consonant with the values of their faith. Deeply personal and instructive, *Holy Ambition* covers an expansive array of topics, providing perspective and the encouragement that it is both possible and deeply rewarding to place values at the center of what one does, how one does it, and who one is in the world."

Kerry Alys Robinson
President and CEO of Catholic Charities USA

"I encourage you to approach this book with intention, whether you are single or married, with or without children. It is a rich tapestry of examples and insights that will guide you through the intricacies of being a

Catholic woman in the workforce. Ultimately, it will leave you inspired to activate your unique gifts and embark on a journey of magnanimity, fearlessly crafting a bold and beautiful life."

From the foreword by Michelle Hillaert
Executive director of the GIVEN Institute

HOLY AMBITION

Thriving as a Catholic Woman at Work and at Home

TARYN DELONG AND ELISE CRAWFORD GALLAGHER

Ave Maria Press AVE Notre Dame, Indiana

Founded in 1865, Ave Maria Press is a ministry of the United States Province of Holy Cross.

www.avemariapress.com

Paperback: 978-1-64680-322-4

E-book: ISBN-13 978-1-64680-323-1

Cover art and text design by Brianna Dombo.

Printed and bound in the United States of America.

Library of Congress Cataloging-in-Publication Data is available.

For my children—
After sainthood, becoming your
mother was my holiest ambition.
—TD

To Rosemary and Emilia—
May you always embrace your
feminine geniuses with strength,
confidence, and an enduring
openness to the Lord's love for you.
—EG

CONTENTS

FOREWORD

Life as a Catholic woman in business looks different for each of us. While some of us have a direct path from high school to college to the business or corporate world, others might have a journey that looks more like hills and valleys, navigating entrepreneurship or corporate work, taking a break from work for one reason or another, and then stepping back in. In this book, Elise and Taryn cover it all and leave you with the profound understanding that, regardless of your path, as a Catholic woman navigating the business world, you're not alone and there is a solid path forward.

As a woman who has experienced the mountains and valleys of business and life, this book resonated with me on every level. As Catholic women navigating business and life, it is often hard, and there are moments when we may feel inadequate, isolated, unseen, or even forgotten, regardless of our vocation in life. I've been through most of it, and this book journeys with you through all of it.

Over the years, life in business has looked different for me depending on where I have been on the journey. Working in the IT industry as a single young woman was exciting, filled with travel, training, and moving up the ranks in a short period of time. I was married in 2000, and then in 2002, when my son was about a year old, I decided to stay home when we moved to Nicaragua for my husband's job. Aside from a brief stint in the late 2000s, I didn't step back into the corporate world and full-time work until 2020.

While staying at home was my calling, it wasn't without its challenges. The desire to do something more burned within me. During those "in-between" years, while building memories with and being present to my children, I did everything from building websites, to branding and design, to building a thriving coaching business—all aimed at keeping my professional profile alive and staying connected with women beyond the confines of my home.

In 2020, I stepped back into the corporate world and in a few short years was directing a business applications team in the disaster industry, flying across the country to help state teams manage eligibility processes through technology. Although I had been absent almost eighteen years from the corporate world, it was as though I hadn't missed a beat. As I read this book, I could relate to the way the authors and contributors navigated these transitions in their personal and professional lives, and especially appreciated the way they addressed the myriad questions that often plague Catholic women in business.

As women striving for holiness, we strive to make all the "right" decisions as we keep our ultimate destination—heaven—in mind. Yet we're not given a clear roadmap, so it's easy to get lost or frustrated or confused. We worry about making the wrong decision, because we just want to get it right. My friend, if there's one thing I've learned over the years, we can't do it alone. We *need* community. It's important to continue to seek mentorship from those who have already learned these lessons and are willing to show us the way.

This book provides answers to questions on ambition, wealth, discernment, relationships, faith, entrepreneurship, and authentic feminine leadership—issues that can weigh heavily on our hearts. We desire to make the right or best decision, but without guidance, it can be easy to be caught up in the fear of making a wrong move or not making any move at all.

In this book, Elise and Taryn share their hearts, guiding you through a maze of uncertainties, stressors, and decisions. This book encapsulates it all, offering insights into making both large and small decisions and sharing tips on how to discern where God is leading you next. It delves into ambition, surrender, wealth, faith, family, entrepreneurship, and the preservation of our feminine identity. Above all, it underscores the importance of embracing leadership and living a magnanimous life.

Reading through these pages, I couldn't help but think, "If only this book had been available when I stepped away from my first job in 2002." I could have read it as a young mom who had just walked away from her career and was sitting in a kiddie pool on our front porch in Nicaragua, eight months pregnant with baby number two, feeling a little lost. It could have been a source of comfort and assurance that this season of life was temporary and given me the courage to trust that God would gradually unveil his plan. Eighteen years later, living out my vocation as a wife, mother, and executive director of the GIVEN Institute, an organization empowering young Catholic female leaders, I recognize the profound gift it is.

I encourage you to approach this book with intention, whether you are single or married, with or without children. It is a rich tapestry of examples and insights that will guide you through the intricacies of being a Catholic woman in the workforce. Ultimately, it will leave you inspired to activate your unique gifts and embark on a journey of magnanimity, fearlessly crafting a bold and beautiful life.

Michelle Hillaert
Executive Director
The GIVEN Institute

INTRODUCTION

WHAT IS WOMEN'S WORK?

> The participation of women in the most diverse professional disciplines could be a blessing for the entire society, private or public, precisely if the specifically feminine ethos would be preserved.[1]
>
> Edith Stein

Elise

In 2017, I founded my first business, a marketing studio named Ringlet. From the start, we were a business "by women and for women." Over the course of seven years, Ringlet grew from a one-woman show to a team of employees all over the United States. We primarily worked with women-owned businesses in the e-commerce, beauty, and restaurant industries.

I felt incredibly blessed to serve our clients. I can't fully describe just how fulfilling it was to watch the Ringlet team unveil new branding to a woman just launching her company or to work with an entrepreneur as we grow her marketing platforms. A new part of each client seemed to come alive when we help her realize her hopes for her business.

I have been asked many times, "Why do you work only with women? Aren't you narrowing your ability to grow your business that way?"

I've thought long and hard about how to answer these questions. And, although it might not sound eloquent or be popular to say, the best answer I've been able to give is, "Women do business differently than men." I've had great experiences working with men in business. However, the reality is that there is a masculine genius and a feminine genius—gifts that come more naturally to men or to women. For example, men tend to be better at compartmentalizing and abstraction,[2] and women tend to be more emotionally intelligent and intuitive (more on these gifts in later chapters). This is not to say that women cannot compartmentalize or think abstractly—or that men are not emotionally intelligent or intuitive. We are speaking in general terms.

The feminine genius resides in every woman, whether she realizes it or not. Women entrepreneurs are fueling economic growth post-pandemic;[3] in the twenty-first century, we have more resources and technology at our fingertips that allow us to work in manners not available to women in previous generations—such as virtually from home or using a flexible schedule.

Taryn

When I was in sixth grade, our social studies class put on a mock European Union event in the evening. Our families came, and I excitedly gave a speech as Margaret Thatcher. I can't remember what I knew about Margaret Thatcher other than that she was the first female prime minister of Great Britain. I can't remember what I said in my speech. But, I do remember how excited I was, as an American, to learn that Great Britain had had a female prime minister.

In tenth-grade civics and economics class, we had to write a report on an entrepreneur. I looked for a female entrepreneur and was excited to learn that the cofounder (with her husband) of Mattel was a woman, Ruth Handler. I can still remember making the title page in pink font, Elle Woods style. It wasn't technically correct, but I figured for a report about the creator of the Barbie doll, it was OK.

In twelfth grade, I decided to go to Meredith College, a small women's college in Raleigh, North Carolina. After touring NC State, UNC–Chapel Hill, and Duke, I decided to apply only to Meredith, which had originally been my backup. Partly, it was out of fear—I felt much safer and much more known at a small campus. In addition, the fact that it was a women's college appealed to me. All of the students spoke about how empowering it was that the leaders in every student organization were female.

I guess you could say I was always going to have a career in supporting and encouraging women. Our media company and online community, Catholic Women in Business—and now this book—is the next step in that journey.

What Is Work?

"Love what you do, and you'll never work a day in your life!" We've all heard some version of this quote, and while it may hold some truth, work is *work*. It's not leisure. It requires effort, skill, time, and energy. Work is not a consequence of the fall. Rather, God designed it for our prosperity and as a means for our sanctification. God created work for us as a way for us to continue his own creation of the earth.

> Then God said, "Let us make man in our image, after our likeness; and let them have dominion over the fish of the sea, and over the birds of the air, and over the cattle, and over all the earth, and over every creeping thing that creeps upon the earth." So God created man in his own image, in the image of God he created him; male and female he created them. (Gn 1:26–27)

We are created in God's image and likeness. Our body, our mind, our talents, our desires, and our thoughts reveal unique traits of God. Our work, therefore, also reveals God's creative power. God is inherently creative; as his image and likeness, we are, too. Work is an expression of our creativity.

Often, when we say "creative," we think of professional artists or our friend who is excellent at home design. But, as St. John Paul II stated in his *Letter to Artists*, we are all called to be creative:

> Not all are called to be artists in the specific sense of the term. Yet, as Genesis has it, all men and women are entrusted with the task of crafting their own life: in a certain sense, they are to make of it a work of art, a masterpiece.

The subject of work can be polarizing, and is often politicized by holding up a particular path as the "ideal" for Catholic women. Naturally, this gives rise to important questions: Is it OK for women to work outside the home? Is it wrong for Catholic women to work for pay? Is there an "ideal" Catholic woman?

These are important questions—and yet, as we can see from scripture and St. John Paul II's direction, work is neither a polarizing choice nor a privilege. Rather, it is our birthright. Through working within our vocational call, we partake in God's generative power and continue his work of creating and caring for the earth (*Laborem Exercens*). Work is not a punishment; it is good. Our work is an unfolding of God's creative power.

We are Catholic moms who have worked in different capacities and in different ways—and have talked with dozens of other women from all walks of life in order to write this book. These fruitful conversations have reminded us of the simple fact that every woman has something to offer the world, whether she works for pay full time, part time, or not at all. In the words of St. John Paul II in his *Letter to Women*:

> Thank you, *women who work*! You are present and active in every area of life-social, economic, cultural, artistic and political. In this way you make an indispensable contribution to the growth of a culture which unites reason and feeling, to a model of life ever open to the sense of "mystery," to the establishment of economic and political structures ever more worthy of humanity.

As we'll discuss in the coming chapters, "Work is love made visible."[4] God has given us the vocation to work so that we can co-create with him and make our own mark on the world. This has been true since the beginning—just listen as Mordecai pleads with his niece, Queen Esther, to take up her royal identity and step into her role in salvation history:

> For if you keep silence at such a time as this, relief and deliverance will rise for the Jews from another quarter, but you and your father's house will perish. And who knows whether

> you have not come to the kingdom for such a time as this? (Est 4:14)

For a time such as this.

Sister in Christ, we, too, are called to take our place in salvation history, and our work is a large part of this mission. As St. John Paul II wrote in *Humanae Vitae* (*On Human Life*), our work is indispensable, not only for others but also for our own faith journey. Work is one of the ways we can encounter Jesus and are transformed by that encounter.

Working as a Woman: A Little "Her-Story"

Until the Industrial Revolution, whether women should work was never in question. Men and women worked in and around the home, both supporting their family in a variety of tasks. Their children stayed with them, babies strapped to mothers and younger children being looked after by older children or other family members.

From the Industrial Revolution (1750–1850) and into the twentieth century, we saw a division of labor in wealthier families: men worked outside the home, while women performed domestic labor (increasingly focused on childcare, as other labor-intensive work was replaced by machines such as dishwashers) inside the home. Legal scholar Erika Bachiochi sums up this change well in an essay for *American Compass*: "As women's work in the home became less quantifiable in economic terms"—in other words, uncompensated—"it also began to lose much of its cultural value."[5]

Meanwhile, in many families, husband and wife both continued to work for pay—but rather than doing so in the home, they were working in factories or in other families' homes. Until child labor laws were passed, many children worked as well. Even with child labor protections, many women had to bring their children to work with them (as some do even today) due to a lack of childcare options.

Now, in the twenty-first-century economy, financial realities are such that few women are able to choose freely between full-time unpaid work in the home and full-time paid work outside the home. Some are forced out of the workforce due to the high cost of (and limited access to) high-quality childcare; others are forced into the workforce due to the high cost of living.

For those families privileged enough to make a choice, there is still an ongoing debate, perhaps especially in Christian circles: Should women—especially mothers—take on work other than caring for home and children? If so, what should that work look like?

Since Elise and I each had our first child in 2021, we have both worked hard to answer these questions for ourselves and our respective families. As our needs and circumstances have changed, the answers have changed as well, from working full time inside the home without childcare to working full time outside the home with childcare. We've both had children on video calls with us and been interrupted by babies and toddlers. We've experienced the challenges and the gifts that come with being a working woman and mother, and we've come to an important conclusion:

There is no one good—or easy—way to do it.

Later in this book, we will explore the process of discernment as well as its application regarding how much (and whether) a woman should work for pay, inside or outside the home. Just as the Church permits each couple to make prudent decisions involving the number and spacing of their children through the use of natural family planning (NFP; *Humanae Vitae*, 10), the Catholic Church leaves the question of whether and how a woman should work up to her own prudential judgment (or, in the case of a married woman, together with her spouse).

Whether single or married, a woman very often has no decision to make: she *must* work to support herself and her household. Other times, the decision may be driven by factors other than financial necessity. For some, the best way to share the talents God has given them is in the business context.

Do Men and Women Work Differently?

Edith Stein, the twentieth-century philosopher, Carmelite nun, and saint known as Teresa Benedicta of the Cross, wrote, "Every profession in which woman's soul comes into its own and which can be formed by woman's soul is an authentic woman's profession."[6] In other words, there are no particular professions that are only men's or only women's professions.

If that's the case, why focus a book on Catholic women in business, rather than on all Catholics in business? Because women have particular strengths, challenges, and ways of working that are worthy of specific attention.

St. John Paul II called the unique strengths of women "the feminine genius" (*Mulieris Dignitatem* [*On the Dignity and Vocation of Women*]) and wrote that "women will increasingly play a part in the solution of the serious problems of the future" (*Letter to Women*).

He said it isn't just "great and famous women of the past or present" who live out the feminine genius in ways that impact the world but also "those *ordinary* women who reveal the gift of their womanhood by placing themselves at the service of others in their everyday lives. For in giving themselves to others each day women fulfill their deepest vocation."

Mothers give themselves to others each day; it's perhaps the easiest example to come to mind. But, in business, women have many opportunities, both small and large, to give themselves to others each day, too. How often have you seen a colleague struggling and encouraged him with a kind word? How often have you gone the extra mile with a client and, perhaps, given her the boost she needed that day? How often have you mentored a less experienced employee and helped her discover and grow her gifts?

Of course, men and women are both called to imitate Jesus in serving rather than being served (Mk 10:45). And yet, in these examples we see the feminine genius at work in a unique way; as St. John Paul II pointed out, "Women *acknowledge the person*, because they see persons with their hearts. . . . They see others in their greatness and limitations; they try to go out to them and *help them*" (*Letter to Women*).

This self-gift can quickly lead to burnout if it is not offered prudently. Our career must involve a continuous process of prayerful discernment. If we serve others without caring for the body and soul that God gave us, we will not be able to be a good steward of the other gifts he gives us—including our relationships with our spouse and family.

With wise stewardship, we can better follow God's call as laywomen and businesswomen.

The Call of the Laity and Your Vocation to Business

So, as Catholic professional women, how are we called to live out our faith today, in "such a time as this"? Wherever you are on your faith journey, this book is for you. Whether you are a recent convert, are rediscovering the faith of your childhood, feel stagnant in your relationship with God, or have always felt at home in the Church, this book is meant to act as a tool for you to encounter a deeper relationship with Jesus and discover a renewed sense of purpose and meaning in your vocation to work and business.

This call to business was planted in your heart for a reason. It is a means for you to become who you were created to be. It's a way to joy and holiness. In the Catholic faith, we describe your "vocation" as your particular calling in this world—your God-given path to heaven. Each one of us is unique, so each of us also has a unique personal vocation, though its goal is the same: holiness. If we are called to marriage, we are called to a holy marriage with a particular person. If we are called to be a mother, we are called to be a particular mother of a particular child or children. As Luke Burgis writes:

> God spoke each creature into existence with a unique word that echoes in its being for all eternity, calling it toward the purpose for which it was created. Every creature receives its being in view of a concrete role. When God creates, He calls.[7]

Every decision that we make, every path we follow, is part of our personal vocation—the way we respond to God's call. If you're reading this book, we're guessing you've discerned that—or are discerning whether—your vocation, at least for a time, includes working in business.

In 1988, St. John Paul II wrote a post-synodal apostolic exhortation reflecting on the events of the Second Vatican Council (1962–1965). This letter, titled *Christifideles Laici* (*Christ's Faithful Laity*), set the standard for the laity of the Church. Pope John XXIII had called the council with the hope that the Church would open wide its doors and usher in a new era of relationship between the faithful laity and religious. St. John Paul II continued this hope throughout his pontificate, especially in his mission to help the laity more profoundly understand their role in salvation history.

In *Christifideles Laici* (*The Lay Members of Christ's Faithful People*), the pope reminds us of our identity as "priest, prophet, and king":

> The participation of the lay faithful in the threefold mission of Christ as Priest, Prophet and King finds its source in the anointing of Baptism, its further development in Confirmation and its realization and dynamic sustenance in the Holy Eucharist. It is a participation given to each member of the lay faithful individually, in as much as each is one of the many who form the one Body of the Lord. . . . The world thus becomes the place and the means for the lay faithful to fulfill their Christian vocation, because the world itself is destined to glorify God the Father in Christ. (2)

As priests, the lay faithful "are united to him (Jesus) and to his sacrifice in the offering they make of themselves and their daily activities." As kings, we are to make a gift of ourselves to serve, "in justice and in charity, Jesus who is himself present in all his brothers and sisters, above all in the very least." Lastly, as prophets, we are "given the ability and responsibility to accept the gospel in faith and proclaim it in word and deed" (*Christifideles Laici*, 14).

Through Baptism, we have access to the Holy Spirit to live out these powerful identities of priest, prophet, and king. St. John Paul II makes it very clear: the call to holiness is not reserved for priests and religious. Our everyday lives as the laity are a means to holiness. Yes, in the endless meetings, the changing of diapers, the answering of emails, the juggling of childcare and dinner planning, you are proclaiming the Gospel, serving in justice and charity, and being Christ's hands and feet in this world.

These seemingly monotonous tasks are holy endeavors. When we unite them to our faith, our work—in business and at home—has an everlasting mark on our soul and the souls of the people around us.

The lay faithful, in fact, "are called by God so that they, led by the spirit of the Gospel, might contribute to the sanctification of the world, as from within like leaven, by fulfilling their own particular duties" (*Christifideles Laici*, 15).

Our duties are not arbitrary. This season of work that you currently are in, whether you are a full-time employee, an entrepreneur, or just getting into (or back into) the workforce, has a purpose. We pray that this book leads you into the next phase of your career with courage, faith, and trust in God.

About This Book

As presidents of Catholic Women in Business, we have a front-row seat to the challenges faced by faithful Catholic women who feel called to business. We wrote this book to help address those challenges. Each chapter asks a question and answers it with insights from our own experiences as well as research from secular and Catholic sources. Online, you can also

find an accompanying study guide, which you can work through on your own or (as we recommend!) with a group of other women. Scan the QR code at left or go to **www.catholicwomeninbusiness.com/holy-ambition** to download that study guide.

Each chapter also includes the story of one female Catholic saint and two contemporary female Catholic business leaders. These leaders started their own businesses or work in organizations begun by others, and they come from a variety of industries, backgrounds, and even continents. Some are mothers; some are married; some are single.

They all have two things in common: they are practicing Catholics, and they feel that God has called them to work in business in some way. They've experienced the challenges we explore in this book, and they have, through a combination of trial and error and grace, found their way through. They all have unique wisdom to share, and we feel privileged to be the vehicle to share it with you.

ONE

CAN CATHOLIC WOMEN BE AMBITIOUS?

> If we think of ambition as an opportunity to invest energy, effort, and imagination into what we value, then it's hard to fathom a list more foundational to how we move through the world, more robust in how it molds and shapes us, and more aspirational than [love, care, community and family].[1]
>
> Rainesford Stauffer, *All the Gold Stars*

Taryn

I always wanted to change the world. I wanted to be a doctor and cure diseases. I wanted to be an author and write the Great American Novel(s). I wanted to lead a massive nonprofit that improved childhood around the globe. I wanted to make the workplace better for women—everywhere. No matter what my career aspirations were, they were always, by any definition of the word, ambitious.

I also had great ambitions for my family and home life. I would get married at twenty-four and have five or six children. I'd continue to play both the piano and the flute. I'd read great books.

In reality, I got married at thirty-one; today, at almost thirty-five, I have a three-year-old and a child in utero. I never became a doctor, and

I don't write fiction, let alone a great novel (although Elise and I have great hopes for this book!). I lead a business with Elise, but a great deal of my time is spent performing the mundane tasks of caring for a small child and a home. I change diapers and potty-train. I cook dinner—often the same boring baked chicken, not a new and exciting recipe.

When I left the full-time workforce, I was thirty-eight weeks pregnant, and the only goal on my mind was having a baby. In the months and years that have passed since then, I've grappled with what it means to be ambitious as a woman who can't succinctly describe what she's currently doing with her time. Am I a stay-at-home mom? A working mom? An entrepreneur? A "mompreneur"? What are my ambitions, and how do they fit into the life God has given me? For that matter, are those ambitions aligned with God's will at all?

Elise

Over my years of adulthood, my definition of ambition and success have vacillated between extremes. In my teens and early twenties, I wanted to be a famous actress on the stage and studied theater in college with hopes of going to Broadway. By graduation, I wanted to be married to my college sweetheart, have children, and be a homeschooling mom.

By his grace, God has led me into some middle ground: I'm a thirty-two-year-old executive working on a hybrid schedule, from home and from an office, with two babies. I have a fire in my belly that keeps me up at night: the desire for greatness and to achieve great things in business. But I also love to do laundry (I know, call me crazy) and find great pride in perfecting my bread recipe.

Ambition is a funny thing. Like Taryn and I have expressed, neither of us fits into the contemporary mold of a "successful" woman. Neither of us has been on the cover of *Forbes* or taken our company public. Our work influences thousands of women online through the Catholic Women in Business blog, Facebook group, and podcast. And yet, both of us value our marriages and motherhood above all else on this earth.

So, where do we go from here? How do we define ourselves as ambitious Catholic women? Is it morally good for us to pursue ambitious goals or dreams?

What Is Ambition?

I can't tell you how many Catholic women have asked me a version of this question: "Elise, I have a desire on my heart to launch a business or apply for a new position at my work or move to a new state . . . do you think I should do it?"

It's so important to make decisions within the context of our vocations, and we'll discuss discernment in another chapter. However, I usually find that the woman asking me that question is really asking me, "Do I have permission to pursue these 'big things' in my life?"

Every woman defines "big things" differently, and the specific goal isn't important here. What is important is that we, as Catholic women, understand what ambition means in the context of our faith.

Sydney King is a Catholic graduate student of international affairs at Johns Hopkins School of Advanced International Studies. Her 2021 article, "Righteous Ambition and the Pursuit of Vocation," explores the idea that for Catholics, ambition looks fundamentally different than how our secular culture defines it. She writes:

> Though righteous ambition serves a similar function of secular ambition, in that it draws humans forward to greater accomplishment, it is, at its core, radically different because of Jesus' teachings. It is noted that "Jesus did not abolish ambition but redefined it. For the ambition to rule others he substituted the ambition to serve others" (Dennis, 2018). Catholic Christians encourage great ambition by asking each Catholic to discern their charisms and vocation, so that they may serve God and His Church in their fullest capacities.[2]

As Catholics, we strive to integrate humility and faithful ambition, which King describes as "other-centered" ambition. The heart of Catholic ambition is the desire to love our God with all of our heart, all of our soul, all of our mind, and all of our strength (Mk 12:28–30). We want to be all that God has created us to be. We want to be fully alive. And our loving Father wants that life for us as well.

Our ambitions, then, should be not just about ourselves. They should encompass others. Our career ambitions should include how we can breathe life into others through our work. Our financial ambitions should include how we can give back to the Church and support people who are less fortunate than ourselves. Our personal ambitions should include goals for our relationships. Our health ambitions should help us care for ourselves and the people we love. And all of our ambitions should be grounded in our relationship with Jesus.

A New Definition of Ambition

For many women, *ambition* has often been a loaded word. There have been research studies—and plenty of anecdotes—over the years supporting the idea that women who are obviously ambitious are often less well-liked than ambitious men. We also have fewer role models in leadership positions and, therefore, less clarity about what career ambitions might look like.

But, in recent years, women have been not only reclaiming ambition but also redefining it. In the 2015 Glamour Women of the Year Gala, actress and media executive Reese Witherspoon said, "I believe ambition is not a dirty word." The speech went viral, and she wrote an essay for *Glamour* two years later, elaborating on the idea. "All we can do to create change is work hard. That's my advice: Just do what you do well. . . . If you are one of those people who has that little voice in the back of her mind saying, 'Maybe I could do [fill in the blank],' don't tell it to be quiet. Give it a little room to grow, and try to find an environment it can grow in."[3]

Are ambitious women out for themselves? Do we climb the ladder or build our business at the expense of other people? Hardly. According to Witherspoon, "We have to do our part to change the idea that a woman with passion and ambition is out only for herself." If more women were ambitious, she wrote, "the world would change."[4]

We asked the women in our Facebook group if they would describe themselves as ambitious. Claire Dwyer (a business leader, editor, and author) said, "Ambition=magnanimity. [I want] to do great things with God for His glory and the good of souls!" Indeed, in his book *Virtuous Leadership: An Agenda for Personal Excellence*, Catholic leadership expert Alexandre Havard emphasizes magnanimity as central to virtuous leadership: "Leaders are magnanimous in their dreams, visions, and sense of mission; in their capacity for hope, confidence, and daring; in their enthusiasm for the effort required to bring their work to a successful conclusion; in their propensity for using means proportionate to their goals; in their capacity to challenge themselves and those around them."[5] Not only is ambition not a dirty word, but it is our calling as Catholics. And our most ambitious calling of all is our calling to be saints.

Saints are people in heaven, whether the Church has officially canonized them or not, "who lived heroically virtuous lives, offered their life for others, or were martyred for the faith, and who are worthy of imitation."[6]

As busy, professional women, why should we seek to mold our lives to examples from people who lived in the past? There are more than ten thousand canonized saints in the Catholic Church. They are men and women who the Church believes are with God in heaven. What greater ambition can we have than to live—and die—like them?

Each chapter in this book will share the life of a saint and the lessons we can take away from her life in our own vocations. We begin with a young woman who sought throughout her life to perform everyday acts with great love.

St. Thérèse of Lisieux and Our Ultimate Ambition

In 1897, a young woman died at her Carmelite convent in Lisieux, France. Her obituary was short, and some of the other nuns reportedly wondered what the obituary writers would put in it; she'd done nothing important.

Today, she is known as St. Thérèse, one of only four female Doctors of the Church. To be declared a Doctor of the Church, someone must be declared so by Church proclamation because of his or her "eminent learning" and "high degree of sanctity."[7] When he declared her a Doctor of the Church, Pope St. John Paul II said:

> Thérèse of Lisieux did not only grasp and describe the profound truth of Love as the center and heart of the Church, but in her short life she lived it intensely. It is precisely this *convergence of doctrine and concrete experience* [emphasis his], of truth and life, of teaching and practice, which shines with particular brightness in this saint, and which makes her an attractive model especially for young people and for those who are seeking true meaning for their life.[8]

Thérèse knew that the highest ambition, the "true meaning" of life, was to be a saint. She had no doubt that she could achieve this ambition because she knew that not only could she not do it on her own, but she didn't have to.

"God cannot inspire unrealizable desires," she wrote. "I can, then, in spite of my littleness, aspire to holiness. . . . I wanted to find an elevator which would raise me to Jesus, for I am too small to climb the rough stairway of perfection."[9] That elevator, she realized, was Jesus himself, and if she became like a small child, he would carry her to sanctity in his arms.

At the end of her life, Thérèse said that she did not want to rest when she reached heaven. It was there that she would fulfill her ultimate ambition as a saint: "My mission is about to begin," she told her sister,

Mother Agnès, "my mission of making God loved as I loved Him, of giving my little way to souls."[10]

As anyone who has received a "rose" from Thérèse will tell you, she has kept her promise. The number of reported miracles, small and large, that have come through Thérèse's intercession is incredible. In 2023, we celebrated 150 years since her birth, and in 2025, we will celebrate 100 years since her canonization. And she is still fulfilling her ambition of sharing Jesus's love with the people who need it most.

Is Burnout Killing Women's Ambition?

We aren't the only ones redefining ambition for ourselves. In 2021, one in three women surveyed by McKinsey & Company said they were considering "downshifting" their career or leaving the workforce, compared to one in four in 2020. Four in ten considered leaving their company or changing jobs, and 42 percent said they were "often" or "almost always burned out" at work in 2021.[11]

During the pandemic, the normal struggle to balance "life" and "work" (as if such things could be separated so neatly) became even more difficult, as many women juggled heightened caregiving responsibilities with their job. Unable to meet all the demands on their time, many women chose to leave full-time work, while others had to leave involuntarily due to layoffs and decreased demand for their work.

Since then, some women have returned to the workforce in similar jobs. Some have decided to be full-time caregivers. Some have opted for more flexible work, part-time work, or entrepreneurship. In fact, several surveys and media outlets have noted that there was a surge in new women-owned businesses during the pandemic.[12]

Could it be that the pandemic simply highlighted needs that many women already had when it came to their careers? Is it possible that not every woman wants the corner office—and that the women who do want it are looking for ways to get there on terms that are more consistent with their values? After all, career coach and author Kathryn Sollmann wrote in 2018, "for decades, women have left these corporate giants because opportunities to work in any flexible way were nonexistent or scarce."[13]

Women leave—but we are still ambitious. A poll of more than five thousand women in the United States in early 2023 found that 48 percent of working women call themselves "very ambitious" about their careers, a small decrease from 54 percent before the pandemic.[14] (The number was 64 percent for Black working women, and 52 percent for Hispanic working women.) Other research, conducted in 2022, found that 48 percent of female leaders who left their organizations in the past two years did so because they wanted more advancement opportunities and that, similarly, 58 percent of women under thirty say career advancement has become more important to them in the past two years.[15] However, many of these women are looking for better work conditions.

Catholic women feel the brunt of unjust and overly demanding workplace policies. Those of us in the workplace who are called to marriage and, often, motherhood, must balance those relationships with the demands of work. We want a purposeful career but don't look to our career for ultimate fulfillment. We seek employment where we don't have to sacrifice our beliefs for our paycheck. We want to lead, and we want to do so in alignment with our values.

Catholic influencer Leah Darrow sparked a movement on Instagram when she started the hashtag #BabiesandDreams from the hospital where she delivered her fifth child. Her post was in response to (then pregnant) actress Michelle Williams's claim in her 2020 Golden Globes speech that she couldn't have achieved her success without abortion. Since then, many other women have used the hashtag to share how they are raising a child or children while building businesses or careers—while others are still working out how on earth those women are doing so.[16]

The Perfectionism Hustle

We live in a hustle culture. So-called "humble brags" about how busy we are serve to demonstrate our importance, and we feel constant pressure to outperform and overachieve. Is it our ambition that's causing us to drive ourselves too hard? Is it the way we can so easily compare ourselves to others on social media? Is it that employers are driving their employees too hard?

At the same time, we are on a never-ending quest for work-life balance, despite the fact that work is part of life and that balance is probably impossible. As psychotherapist Katherine Morgan Schafler writes, "Balance remains one step ahead, the ever-elusive prize of female modernity"—yet "I don't know one balanced woman."[17] She adds that women's ambition is too often labeled and pathologized as "perfectionism."

How can we differentiate between what Morgan Schafler calls "maladaptive perfectionism" and healthy ambition? For Catholics, it comes down to two questions: what is your ambition, and why? If your ambition is rooted in dreams that God has placed in your heart, and you are striving to achieve that ambition with his help, that can be healthy. If your ambitions are rooted in worldly measures of success, or you are striving to achieve goals on your own, without God's help, that can be unhealthy.

Taryn

My perfectionism tends to be rooted in my social anxiety and in the sin of pride. I want to be perfect—and I want everyone to know it! Becoming a mother forced me to finally come to terms with my perfectionism. I wanted to be a mother who never made mistakes, and I wanted everyone I came in contact with to think I was a good mother (whatever that means). I had to realize eventually, though, that I could only be a good mother with God's help, and I certainly couldn't be a perfect one. Growing in humility has helped me to become less of a perfectionist.

I still have ambition, though. Of course, I still want to be a good mother. I want to be a good writer and a good leader. But, I want to do those things with God's help and only because I've discerned that he wants me to set those goals.

I also want to note that too often, perfectionism can be driven by external pressure. Whether it's a boss with unrealistic expectations or the pressure to put food on the table or pay off student loans, we live in an economy that can be stressful at best and unsustainable at worst. Know that if you are in this place, you are not alone. We've been there, and so have countless other women. It's key to set boundaries and look for work that helps you maintain your prayer life and your health. (More on this topic later!)

Elise

I have thrown out the idea of balance over the past three years. Between running several businesses during a pandemic, having two babies in two years, and mourning difficult family dynamics, I realized that "balance" was never going to happen for me in this season of life. And, frankly, striving to constantly strike a "balance" between all of these things and measuring myself against how well I'm achieving that "balance" is exhausting.

The concept that has resonated with me the most is the idea of "flow." The goal on a daily, weekly, and monthly basis is not to "balance" work, family, marriage, faith, friendships, hobbies, and passions. I have to begin by accepting my weaknesses and limitedness. Like Taryn, I struggle with pride and the belief that I can "do it all." I simply can't. Choosing to work outside of the home right now in order to provide financially for my family comes with heartbreaking sacrifices. However, the Lord has reassured me that this is where he is calling me in this season of life. I know when I'm investing in my home life that my friendships might not be as abundant as they were in my early twenties. All of these different seasons are blessed and sanctified by my heavenly Father.

I'd like us as women to take one deep, collective breath and let go of the incredible pressures that we put upon ourselves. We need to steel ourselves against impulsively chasing the cultural and moral ideals for women that have been communicated to us since childhood. Instead, we need to quiet ourselves and attune our hearts to the voice of God in order to receive our true callings, letting go of whatever is holding us back from accepting the Lord's will in our lives.

The Pandemic and the End of "Girlbossdom"

The term "girlboss" was popularized by Sophia Amoruso, founder of Nasty Gal, in her 2014 book *#Girlboss*. It was used to denote female empowerment, particularly in the business context. However, in recent years, as we touched on in the introduction, it's come under criticism for a connotation of toxic hustle culture and an exclusion of non-white women.

Some women have also criticized it for the use of the word "girl," saying that using a gender qualifier is infantilizing.[18] We would argue that if that's the case, #womanboss should be fine—we should feel empowered by our sex, not patronized. Feminizing leadership isn't a problem, but promoting a single idea of what feminine leadership looks like is.

My (Elise's) early career was heavily influenced by and seeped in "girl boss-dom." I graduated college in 2013; earned my master's in 2015; and started my first company, Ringlet, in 2016. These years were the height of Sophia Amoruso's influence. Women were starting businesses left and right. Amoruso and other women like her (e.g., Whitney Wolfe Herd of Bumble and Zooey Deschanel of HelloGiggles) were unlike any other business leaders I had ever seen: they embraced their femininity in the boardroom, wore pink, and were unapologetic about their ambition.

I started Ringlet with just a few business connections, a laptop, and a move back into my mom's house to save money. Over my first five years, my business slowly grew from a one-woman show to a business with part-time employees, interns, and, eventually, four full-time employees. We had a beautiful office in Washington, DC, and we were serving clients around the world.

Then, the COVID-19 pandemic hit. I distinctly remember the last meeting we had in our office before we decided to pause in-person meetings. The meeting was with a mother-daughter team that was starting a travel agency. My team met with them to create a business plan and marketing strategy for their launch. I remember feeling so fulfilled and proud of the work we created in that meeting. I knew that the plans we drafted would propel our clients into making their dreams a reality.

As mid-March 2020 moved into early summer 2020 and we continued to pivot our business model, I'm proud to say that Ringlet survived the pandemic. Our team worked from home and continued to produce great work for our clients.

However, during the pandemic, my life changed greatly. I got pregnant with our first daughter in July 2020 and experienced undiagnosed hyperemesis gravidarum (severe morning sickness) for the majority of my pregnancy. My lifestyle drastically changed, from not only abiding by distancing practices to avoid COVID but also just trying to survive on a day-to-day basis in order to care for my mental and physical health. I was grateful for my business partner, Claire Conway, who stepped into a COO role to run our company.

We welcomed Rosemary Ann in March 2021 and were surprised by another pregnancy in the fall of 2021. After another challenging pregnancy, I gave birth to our second daughter, Emilia Jane, in June 2022.

By that summer, Ringlet had undergone a tremendous transformation from the company I had started in 2016. We had taken on investors in the previous years and decided to reduce the number of our employees and shift our business model. Now that I was a mom of two, the Lord was calling me to reexamine how I defined success and ambition. Over the seven years I'd run Ringlet, my prayer had consistently been, "Lord, this is your business. If you want me to continue, please give me the strength to do so. If you don't, please make it abundantly clear that it's time to step away."

For so many years, I tied my identity to growing Ringlet. Now, my world had broadened through marriage and motherhood. I still felt called to work, but I no longer could—or wanted to—give the same attention to Ringlet as I did before. I was in a different season of life. My definition of ambition moved from impacting colleagues and clients through business to creating a domestic church for my family.

For other women across the globe, the chaos of the pandemic similarly shifted their view of ambition. As *The Cut* columnist Amil Niazi wrote in her article "Losing My Ambition," "By the time I was parenting a toddler and a newborn in lockdown, my idea of ambition had been permanently altered. I had to keep working to keep everyone fed and alive, and I realized I didn't want or need more than that. I wasn't willing to give up any more mental or emotional space to the idea that work itself was the pathway to something more. Work wasn't my identity or my family; it was a means to an end."[19]

For many millennial-age women, the pandemic was a wake-up call. The siren of being a girl boss, one who does it all, came to a screeching halt. We were forced to rethink how we defined ourselves as working women and, for many of us, wives and mothers. Additionally, we realized how narrow the "girl-boss" movement was. Striving to be an entrepreneur or having flexibility to change jobs isn't an option for most women.

Caroline Kenagy, an ambitious young businesswoman, strives for the flexibility to adjust course according to God's plan.

Caroline Kenagy: Early Career Ambition

Caroline Kenagy joined Catholic Women in Business as an intern while she was a student at the University of Kansas; she later became our community manager. Caroline is also an associate marketing manager for a medical equipment manufacturing company, where she feels like she's working toward a greater purpose of helping to save lives.

Caroline considers herself ambitious, but she thinks that ambition can take over someone's life. She struggles with perfectionism and has to regularly set boundaries for herself. "There's a line between being ambitious and being OK with not reaching your goal the way that you . . . envisioned it to be," she said. "I get really clear plans in my head, and I get attached to those plans, and if they don't unfold the way that I thought they should unfold, I get really frustrated."

"It's a matter of trusting that you're where God wants you to be," Caroline noted, and "coworking with God, asking him what he wants for your life, whether that's in a career or in a relationship or whatever it may be. And I think just really listening to him and being open to [something that] might not be what you want, but it's what he wants."

When it comes to looking to the future, to having a family and professional ambitions, Caroline said that she's been able to see recently that "you don't have to choose one." The two paths are not mutually exclusive. "I did fear that," she said, "but being part of Catholic Women in Business has shown me that it's possible [to have both]."

Receiving Your Identity and Knowing Your Worth

Postpandemic, we hope that society is evolving to a more Catholic view of work: that it is not meant to encompass our entire identity but, rather, is a means to make a living and is a part of our path to holiness. It is one part of our vocation, enabling us to give of ourselves in the way we are called in order to become the women God calls us to be.

Where do you place the most emphasis when it comes to your self-worth? Do you identify most in terms of your relationships with other people—maybe as a daughter, wife, sister, friend, or mother? Do you identify most in terms of your career? Especially for those of us for whom our career is a calling, it can be tempting to place our entire identity in it.

As Christians, our universal call is "to know [God], to love him with all [our] strength" (*CCC* 1). Foremost among any other role we play in our life is our identity as a daughter of God. All of your worth—everything that makes you good and beautiful—comes from the fact that you are loved by God and made in his image.

So, yes, maybe you are also a talented designer or an empathetic manager or a visionary leader or an astute accountant. But you are those things because God made you that way and because you are stewarding the gifts he gave you.

This is not to downplay your talents—it is to celebrate them and help you prioritize them. It is also a reminder that when you inevitably make a mistake, whether it's a small typo in an ad you're copyediting or a bad deal that lost your company tens of thousands of dollars, that mistake has nothing to do with who you are. You are a daughter of a God who has counted every hair on your head (Lk 12:7). You can never do anything to deserve his love—and you can never do anything to lose it.

Addressing Imposter Syndrome

Imposter syndrome is an experience of self-doubt and a fear that others will find out you are an "imposter"—that you aren't as gifted as you seem. The psychologists (women themselves) who coined the term in the 1970s identified it among high-achieving women.[20] While both sexes experience imposter syndrome, the fact that women have fewer female role models among business leaders and have historically experienced barriers to business success can create this type of identity crisis among women climbing the ladder.[21]

While everyone can work to change the workplace to solve the systemic problems that contribute to imposter syndrome in women, there are some approaches we can take for ourselves, too. *Psychology Today* recommends reflecting on your achievements, talking about your imposter syndrome with someone who cares about you, going into new experiences expecting to make mistakes (it's a learning process!), and looking for a mentor.[22] Remember, you have carefully discerned your career decisions, and you are not an imposter—you are a beloved daughter of God, stewarding the gifts that he gave you.

How Do You Define Success?

There are many, many methods, systems, and "best practices" for setting goals. From New Year's resolutions to quarterly objectives, from SMART goals[23] to BHAG goals,[24] from OKRs to KPIs,[25] it seems that every personal development expert over the last hundred years has published a new "ideal" way to set goals and evaluate success.

What matters most for us as Catholic businesswomen, though, is whether we are setting goals that (a) are aligned with our values and (b) are aligned with what we believe to be God's will for us. The first part comes from prayerful reflection on what's important to you; the second, from prayerful discernment, which we'll discuss in the next chapter.

So, what are your top priorities? Is the way you spend your time aligned with those priorities? Sometimes, of course, we don't have a choice about how we spend our time; most people have to work at least eight hours a day in order to pay the bills. But, what about outside of that time? Are you pursuing goals that are aligned with what you believe to be most important?

In her book *The Myth of the Nice Girl*, investor and former media executive Fran Hauser writes that "true success comes from when you use your talents and your genuine kindness to do work that is aligned with your values and passions."[26] You get to define what success means to you. Maybe it's a corner office and a C-suite title. Maybe it's a successful side gig while you care full time for your child or children. Maybe it's something in between. It's up to you—and God.

Success is going to look different in each season of our lives. It might even change from day to day! I (Elise) used to love setting yearly and quarterly goals, and I still do! But now, some of my goals look different. They may be as simple as showering and making sure everyone is fed and sleeping after welcoming a new baby into our family. Or they may be getting through an intense time of business, such as the end of a fiscal year.

Whatever our definition of success may look like on any given week, it's important that we give ourselves permission for that definition to change often. Success is not static; it's fluid. Our ultimate goal, though, is always holiness.

Glory Enyinnaya explains how, on her path to holiness, she always keeps God's will in mind.

Glory Enyinnaya: Finding Truth and Seeking Sainthood

Glory Enyinnaya is the founder of Kleos Africa, a consulting firm that supports entrepreneurship in Africa through partnerships with the continent's largest banks. She earned a doctorate in management in 2023, and her research on entrepreneurship has been published in the *Harvard Business Review*. She also teaches at Lagos Business School and Pan-Atlantic University and is "passionate about female empowerment."

"I believe in the vocational nature of work, and I see my work not as a burden, but as an intrinsic part of my purpose and calling as a Catholic Christian," Glory said. "As a Christian, I believe the virtue of charity refines and redirects ambition from a focus on solely gratifying one's needs to a focus on glorifying God and meeting the needs of others alongside one's legitimate needs."

Part of what's helped Glory see the value of work from a Catholic perspective is becoming a cooperator in Opus Dei. "I have come to view my work as a means of glorifying God, striving to integrate principles of diligence, integrity, and service into every aspect of my professional life," she said. "This spiritual framework has instilled in me a commitment to excellence and moral integrity, allowing me to nurture a culture of ethical leadership and holistic growth within my entrepreneurial ventures and educational initiatives."

Glory hasn't always had this approach to ambition. "As a young person, I was ambitious for professional success," she said. "However, my mother's demise brought home the transitory nature of earthly achievements, and I began to long for something more transcendental. This led to my conversion to Catholicism.

"Slowly, but inexorably, my focus has changed from achieving fame and fortune to pleasing God," Glory said. "My life's ambition now is to be a saint . . . [and] I try to make this the center and organizing principle of my life." Part of keeping her work other-focused rather than self-focused involves serving as a mentor in programs such as the Cherie Blair Foundation for Women, the African Women Entrepreneurship Cooperative, She Leads Africa, and Flourish Africa.

"I view my talents, resources, and opportunities as gifts from God," Glory said. "As a steward, I aim to use these blessings wisely and for the greater good in pursuing my goals." While she has a process that she follows when setting those goals, she believes it's important to remain flexible in order to follow God's will, even if it leads her to unexpected places.

What About Failure?

Sooner or later, each of us will inevitably fail to achieve a goal. Sometimes, the setback is only temporary; for example, it took us a couple of tries to write a book proposal that would green-light a contract with our publisher. When you don't succeed the first time, you can try again, learning from that failure, or you can reevaluate: Is that goal still something that you believe is important to your career, your life, and, ultimately, your path to sanctity? (Not every goal will be directly related to pursuing holiness—but each should, at the very least, not block that path.)

Our goals may also change over time. It's important not to hold onto goals too tightly. With a loose grip, you leave room for the Holy Spirit. I (Taryn) previously had career goals of being a teacher and then being a nonprofit manager. Now, I'm a professional writer, editor, and business leader. I feel happier and more on track with God's plan for my life than I ever did before, but I can still see God's hand on the windy path I took to arrive here. I teach—not children, but adults—by writing and mentoring other Catholic businesswomen. I use the skills I learned in my graduate coursework to manage Catholic Women in Business operations with Elise.

It would be easy to say that I should have stuck to my original goals. After all, I spent a lot of money on tuition to work toward those goals—why should I give up? But, by listening to what I would have then called my intuition and what I now realize was the Holy Spirit, I opened up so much more possibility for my life. By following this new path, I am able to make a much bigger impact than I could have previously, because I am more fully aligned with God's plan and using the gifts that he gave me.

Dropping out of student teaching my senior year of college and leaving graduate school halfway through a master's program doesn't look good on a resume and doesn't sound good in an interview. But, sometimes saying "yes" to God means saying "no" to something the world would tell you is important.

Of course, that doesn't mean you won't have mixed feelings about making the change. As I decided to stop Ringlet operations in early 2023, I (Elise) had a moment (OK, multiple moments!) of fear. "If I shut down my company, what does it say about me? What will people think? Am I a failure?"

Eventually, I realized that I am still Elise, even if I step away from Ringlet—or even from my career. Stepping away doesn't negate the years of learning and knowledge I gained running Ringlet. I stewarded the business as I was called, for as long as I was called. I responded to the Lord and received his will for me and, in doing so, allowed the experience to form me and discovered more of myself. That, in and of itself, is a success.

Questions for Reflection and Discussion

1. What feelings does the word "ambition" bring up for you? Would you describe yourself as an ambitious person? Why or why not?
2. What are your career ambitions? What ambitions do you have for other areas of your life?
3. Where does your identity come from? Do you struggle to see yourself first and foremost as a daughter of God? What can you do to remind yourself from day to day that you are beloved?
4. Have you ever felt like an imposter at work? What did you do to overcome that feeling?
5. How do you define success? Think of a time you set a big goal for yourself. Did you reach it? Why or why not?
6. Do you have a favorite saint? How does he or she inspire your ambition to be a saint?

TWO

HOW DO I DISCERN AND SURRENDER TO GOD'S WILL FOR MY CAREER?

> Great decision-making isn't a single skill—it involves many skills. You have to be able to clarify your purpose, come up with many options, analyze those options, test your assumptions, select the option that matches your top priorities, generate buy-in, and prepare for what happens if you're wrong. Both men and women can acquire all of these skills, but . . . a few of them come more easily to women.[1]
>
> Therese Huston, *How Women Decide*

Taryn

I loved my job. I'd been working at the same company for six years, and I was good at what I did. I'd been promoted twice. My coworkers were fantastic, the work was interesting and engaging, and I had a fair and kind boss. I was even, according to Glassdoor, paid above my "market value."

So, why was I longing to leave?

I'd thought for a while that I would be a full-time working mom when my husband and I had children, partly for financial reasons and partly because, as I said, I loved my job. But, as my pregnancy progressed, I felt a deep tug in my heart to quit working full time to care for our daughter.

This change in my desires was inconvenient, to say the least; we were pretty sure our budget would not allow us to lose my salary. So, we started to pray about it. I called on my longtime spiritual father, St. Joseph, whose intercession has changed my life in several beautiful ways. Was I being called to care for my daughter full time? Was it even feasible?

One morning, I woke up early with a shocking feeling of peace. I tend to be an anxious person; peace does not come naturally to me, so this feeling was strange and overwhelming. I knew that God was asking me to quit my job, and I knew that he was going to find a way for us to make it work.

I write this as my daughter is asleep. We spend our days together; I work while she naps and after she goes to bed, sometimes answering an email or taking a Zoom meeting while she plays (or adds to the conversation).

It's clear why God called me down this part-time work-from-home path. It's just right for my temperament, our family's needs, and even for my career, which has, strangely enough, taken off since I quit working full time. Will it always be right for us? I don't know—but I do know that we are trying to stay receptive enough to hear if God calls us down a different path.

Receiving God's Will

Discernment requires a posture of receptivity—an openness to listening to God. This receptivity often conjures images of passivity, of women who simply let things happen to them without having any agency. But this image is not a Catholic conception of feminine receptivity. Consider, instead, a different image:

A woman finds out that friends have run out of wine at a wedding reception. Concerned at the embarrassment that they will experience having no wine to serve their guests, she goes to her son, who she knows can work miracles, and asks him to do something about it.

"O woman, what have you to do with me?" He responds. "My hour has not yet come" (Jn 2:4).

The woman tells the servers to do whatever he tells them to do. And he turns water into wine.

Mary was not a passive woman—but she was a receptive one. She took action when needed, but the gospels tell us that she was also constantly listening for God's voice and letting him work in her life. She was bold enough to tell Jesus that something needed to be done, and she was humble enough to listen to his response. We are called to do the same.

In her book *The Privilege of Being a Woman*, philosopher Alice von Hildebrand writes that receptivity "is not to be confused with passivity, as Aristotle does when he claims that the male is superior to the female because he is 'active,' whereas she is passive." She says that receptivity is "alert, awakened, joyful readiness." Men and women are both receptive, because all that we have is a gift from God, but "women feel at home in this receptivity and move in it with ease and grace."[2]

By receiving God, we understand and use the gifts he gave us, and by receiving others, we nurture and care for them. As Catholic speaker and author Danielle Bean said in a 2019 interview with *Angelus News*, "Receptivity is where relationship begins, and it's inside of relationship with God and with others, that we do our most meaningful work."[3]

We are receptive when we attempt to discern God's will for our life and our career; when we surrender to that will; when we steward the gifts we receive from God; and when we receive our identity and our worth from God, not the world. This is the lesson Alexandra Macey Davis learned in her path of discernment.

Alexandra Macey Davis: Following God's Plan Alone

Alexandra Macey Davis is a mother and the managing editor of *Public Discourse*. She previously worked as a litigation attorney for two years in an ideal situation, yet she wasn't happy. As a result, she learned that it's not selfish to discern a better fit. That transition is "very uncomfortable and very overwhelming," but it's worth it.

Because of her degree in English, Alexandra had been doing a lot of marketing for her firm. She started looking into content marketing as a career and realized that as someone who was both a lawyer and a writer, she could be a huge asset to law firms.

"I thought, 'This is kind of a confluence of a lot of things that I think are strengths of mine, so I wonder what it would look like,'" she said. "And I feel like that's how every clear transition I've had has started: 'I wonder what it would look like if I could try it.'" So she launched her business, Davis Legal Media.

Five years later, Alexandra had two children and was scaling down the business when two of her favorite online publications announced that they were looking for a managing editor. "I cannot explain why," she said. "I was not looking for a job, but I applied to both. And, long story short, the *Public Discourse* one . . . just kind of fell into my lap." After a lot of prayerful discernment, she determined taking the job was the right path.

We asked Alexandra what she does to hear God's voice, and the first thing she said was going to adoration. If she can't make it to adoration, if she's feeling "frenzied," she pulls up the adoration livestream from EWTN's website. She also delves into spiritual reading, talks to friends "who are also really seeking the Lord," and has started going to Confession more frequently.

"In seasons where I am so much more deliberate about speaking to the Lord and trying to hear from him," Alexandra said, "I do see a lot more fruit."

Discernment: Decision-Making with God

Often, when we hear the word "discernment," we think of the process of discerning marriage or religious life. But we use discernment anytime we have an important decision to make. Christian discernment goes beyond a pro-con list (although it's not a bad starting place!). It's not just deciding what we want; it's being receptive to what God wants for us.

In a 2022 general audience, Pope Francis described discernment as "that reflection of the mind, of the heart, that we have to do before making a decision." He said that discernment requires knowledge, experience, emotion, will, and hard work. It requires self-awareness—knowing what is good for you. Most of all, he said, "it requires a filial relationship with God."[4]

In other words, to discern well, we must have a father/daughter relationship with God. We must look to him for guidance, for encouragement. God is more loving than the best earthly father—he gives us everything we need without forcing his will. We can discern his will, but it is our choice to follow it.

This process of discernment is obviously important when it comes to major life decisions like whether to get married. But one thing we know about God is that he cares about every part of life. He doesn't just have a plan for our "big V" vocation—he has a plan for our vocation to business as well. Business can be a calling from God, which means that prayerful discernment is important here, too.

Understanding Women's Intuition

"Women's intuition" is a phrase commonly used for a woman's ability to quickly understand and respond to people's emotions, and women are commonly thought to make decisions based on intuition. Is it wrong to make decisions this way? Could intuition actually be the Holy Spirit? And is it true that women are more likely to make decisions based on their "gut" than men are? It's certainly true for my (Taryn's) husband and me! He sometimes has to ask me to slow down so we can talk things through.

In her book *How Women Decide*, psychologist Therese Huston examines the research on questions like these. Many of the stereotypes are just that—stereotypes. However, Huston did find that women have some unique strengths when it comes to making decisions:

1. *Women tend to be intuitive when it comes to emotions—our own and others'* (more on this in chapter 4).
2. *Women tend to be more likely to seek advice* when making an important decision—in other words, we are more receptive to others!
3. *Women tend to be more accurate in our self-assessments and less prone to overconfidence*, helping us make prudent decisions. Perhaps this inclination toward modesty is a driver in our receptivity to feedback.
4. *Under stress, women tend to opt for smaller but less risky choices.* Men, on the other hand, tend to make decisions that are riskier but would have a bigger payout if they turn out well. Huston concludes that especially in times of stress, organizations need both men and women making decisions (an argument for the Catholic idea of complementarity, which we will explore in chapter 8).

"We may savor the idea of a man of action," Huston writes, "but we should also value a woman of discernment."[5]

Surrendering Your Career to the Lord

Elise

In February 2023, I went through a major career discernment process. I had been building my first company, Ringlet, for seven years but was facing severe burnout. After two pregnancies and births during the pandemic and running a company during those changes, I was ready for something new. My husband and I had moved from the Washington, DC, area to the Baltimore area, which brought us closer to family—and to my family's business, JC Law. My father started the firm thirty years ago, but it grew from a fifteen-person firm in 2019 to an eighty-five-person firm in 2023. My husband clerked for the firm during law school and began his career as a domestic defense attorney at the firm in the summer of 2022.

When I was first presented with the possibility of working at JC Law at the beginning of 2023, I was resistant to the idea. Ten years earlier, I had specifically chosen not to go to law school, because I didn't want to be a lawyer. The idea of working with lawyers seemed counterintuitive. Plus, I had just devoted my twenties to building a company, network, and reputation in DC as a CEO. Who would I be without Ringlet?

However, as I spoke with my Ringlet cofounder, Claire, and my husband, I slowly became more open to this change. A step during this discernment process that aided my decision-making was spending three months taking JC Law on as a client. This allowed me to run my team at Ringlet while getting acquainted with the JC Law staff, learning the back end of the company, and beginning to envision what my role at the firm would look like.

Eventually, Claire and I decided to sell Ringlet. I'm slowly beginning to see why the Lord prompted me to make this shift. I have been thrust into a new level of leadership and responsibility at JC Law that I've never experienced before, and it has stretched me and forced me to learn new skills. This shift has also been fruitful for our family. Although I am out of the house more than I was before, the increased separation between work and home has allowed me to be more attentive to my daughters when I am home.

This time has reaffirmed my identity in Christ. In letting go of Ringlet, I received in a deeper way my identity as his daughter. It is not my work that gives my life purpose; it is my life with and in him. In the past year, this scripture has come up often:

> For everything there is a season, and a time for every matter under heaven: a time to be born, and a time to die; a time to plant, and a time to pluck up what is planted; a time to kill, and a time to heal; a time to break down, and a time to build up; a time to weep, and a time to laugh; a time to mourn, and a time to dance; a time to cast away stones, and a time to gather stones together; a time to embrace, and a time to refrain from embracing; a time to seek, and a time to lose; a time to keep, and a time to cast away; a time to tear, and a time to sew; a time to keep silence, and a time to speak; a time to love, and a time to hate; a time for war, and a time for peace. (Eccl 3:1–8)

Being a working professional over the past ten years has taught me that my life and career will have seasons. It is not static. Long gone are the days when people stayed at one company for forty-plus years! But, more than that, my life will continue to change as our family life shifts and changes as well.

As a working mom, my current state in life requires daily and even hourly discernment. With a one-year-old and two-year-old who are changing quickly, I have to constantly discern where my time and attention are needed. As I manage almost a hundred people at work and lead our scaling efforts across states—while prioritizing my vocations as wife, mother, and homemaker—it's easy for me to become overwhelmed. There are a lot of people asking me questions or needing something from me.

However, when I submit my time to Jesus in prayer, I receive the energy and wisdom I need to stand in front of the demands of my life with grace and courage. This can look as simple as closing my eyes in my office for three minutes before a meeting to ask the Holy Spirit to guide my words or pausing before I go into the house to do a breathing exercise and let go of whatever happened at work that day.

Surrendering your career to the Lord is not a one-time event. It is a season-by-season, day-by-day, hour-by-hour process. It is the Lord's hope that through this discernment, we learn to trust him more genuinely and allow our vision of ourselves to expand, as Stacey Sumereau reminds us.

Stacey Sumereau: Surrendering to God's Dramatic Plans

Stacey Sumereau is a mother of four; a candlemaker; and a Catholic speaker and singer known for her podcast, *Called and Caffeinated*. She started her career as a Broadway actress, performing on two national tours before discerning religious life on the Lifetime TV show *The Sisterhood: Becoming Nuns*.

Stacey ultimately discerned that she was called to marriage and launched her podcast in the midst of having her first two children. "I feel like the Lord likes to use me in very sudden, dramatic ways, and then everything changes," Stacey told us. For example, after needing to turn down an opportunity to publish a book, the lockdowns of spring 2020 happened, and she hosted an online conference (the first of its kind). She prepared for it in a matter of days and helped almost twenty thousand people around the world get through those dark early days of the pandemic. By telling her "no" to the book, Stacey said, "God was really clearing the path so that he could put something better in the way." (She is now writing a book for Ave Maria Press on discernment, to be released in spring 2025.)

In 2021, Stacey had an emergency C-section with her third baby. She and the baby almost died, and her daughter was in the NICU for four months. It was a time of intense suffering, but Stacey said, "This is the experience that I needed to have in order to . . . shake me out of this selfishness."

It also helped her realize that she'd always struggled with identifying her worth in terms of her productivity and her work. "There's this temptation for me to over-identify myself with my achievements," she said. "The NICU really made me understand that that's not where it's at."

Stacey defines receptivity as a form of surrender: "holding your hands loosely so that God can actually give you something greater." She said that it also means accepting the gifts that he has given her and not envying someone else's. The Lord is creative—he gives each person unique gifts for a unique purpose. When we read scripture regularly, we can recognize his voice, and we can listen for him to share his plan for us. After all, Stacey noted, "he cares more about you than about the success of your business."

Taryn

Several years ago, I learned to surrender control by participating in a national initiative that gathered leaders from nonprofit organizations, government agencies, and employers to discuss the state of disability employment in the United States. It was an exciting project that culminated in a report that I edited and a presentation and press event, at which I was invited to speak on a panel.

Several days before the presentation, which was in DC, I caught the flu. I prepared for the panel feverishly (literally) while blowing my nose, popping zinc tablets, and taking Tamiflu. Eventually, though, I had to admit that I was not going to be well enough to get on a plane, let alone speak in public, and I had to give them enough notice to find someone to replace me.

I was crestfallen—I'd been so excited for this presentation. My husband, who was then my fiancé, comforted me, telling me there would be other opportunities in my career and that this was a good lesson in detachment and surrender. Clearly, God did not want me in DC that day—or in the office for the next two weeks, during which my flu turned into pneumonia.

Did I mention this was February 2020?

I was back in the office for four days when they sent us home to work remotely. Ultimately, I never went back—and the entire world spent the next couple of years learning to surrender to things that were out of our control.

We all experience career setbacks. Edith Stein was not allowed to be a professor because she was a woman and, later, because she was Jewish. (This experience can make her a great intercessor for women who experience bias in the corporate world today.) Then, after her conversion, she immediately felt called to join the Carmelite Order. However, she was discouraged from doing so for eleven years.

Despite these obstacles and delays, Edith fully lived her feminine genius, even in ways that she had not anticipated. She was unable to enter religious life, but she wrote articles contributing to the field of philosophy, taught German and history, and spoke extensively on women's issues. Today, she is a canonized saint, and the work she did during those eleven years continues to inspire and teach us. As she wrote:

> Things were in God's plan which I had not planned at all. I am coming to the living faith and conviction that—from God's point of view—there is no chance and that the whole of my life, down to every detail, has been mapped out in God's

> divine providence and makes complete and perfect sense in God's all-seeing eyes.[6]

Learning to surrender to God's will is a long, hard road. Some people learn it the hard way, through crises that try our faith, our relationships, and our mental or physical health. Some learn it through practice, gradually learning to loosen our tight grip on our lives and our careers and hand them over to Jesus.

Rethinking Time Management

The phrase "time management" implies that we have ownership over our time—that we have full control over it. When we see our time as a gift, we start to use it more wisely—to *steward* it rather than *manage* it. By organizing our schedule through the lens of time stewardship rather than time management, we identify our priorities and order our lives accordingly.

Take a look inside many organizations, and you'll see that many of us have turned work and productivity into an idol. The consequence is the well-known phenomenon of "hustle culture," with long work hours and many personal sacrifices. We'll never be able to finish everything we want to finish, and we'll never accomplish every goal—but we aren't meant to. With a time-stewardship mindset, we know that God calls us to cooperate with him in his work, not do it all for him. As Fr. (later Bishop) Ken Untener wrote, "We accomplish in our lifetime only a tiny fraction of the magnificent enterprise that is God's work. . . . No set of goals and objectives includes everything."[7]

As Catholics, we often talk about how we live in a consumerist society, but we may not always be aware of the ways consumerism can seep into other areas of life. Just as we must be careful stewards of the treasure God has given us (more on that in the next chapter!), we must also be careful stewards of our time.

Hustle culture treats time as a commodity that we never have enough of. We must constantly spend it in order to feel that we are valuable—but as Christians, we know that we aren't valuable because of what we do or what we produce. We're valuable because we are daughters of God, made in his image.

Do I really need to check my email right now? Perhaps—I might be waiting on a message that needs immediate action. Or I may simply need to be present at that particular moment to my husband, child, or parent or a coworker or friend. It may be that the email can wait. By examining our time with the mindset of a steward rather than a hustler, we can better determine how we should be using it.

Stewarding God's Other Gifts

God gives us many gifts, and as Christians—men or women—we are called to receive and use them wisely. At Baptism, and even more so at Confirmation, we receive the gifts of the Holy Spirit, which "are permanent dispositions which make man docile in following the promptings of the Holy Spirit" and sustain our moral life (*CCC* 1830). The Church teaches that there are seven gifts: "wisdom, understanding, counsel, fortitude, knowledge, piety, and fear of the Lord" (*CCC* 1831). There are also nine fruits of the Spirit, found in Galatians 5:22–23: love, joy, peace, patience, kindness, goodness, faithfulness, gentleness, and self-control (*CCC* 1832).

The gifts and fruits of the Holy Spirit help us become more receptive to our charisms, "'special graces among the faithful of every rank' for the building up of the Church" (*CCC* 951). In other words, these charisms are given to us by the Holy Spirit specifically for the purpose of serving others. The Catherine of Siena Institute identifies twenty-four common charisms,[8] based on lists provided in St. Paul's letters as well as the writings of St. Thomas Aquinas:

- Pastoral charisms: encouragement, hospitality, helping, pastoring, and mercy
- Communication charisms: evangelism, prophecy, and teaching
- Organizational charisms: giving, leadership, service, and administration
- Healing charisms: healing and intercessory prayer

- Understanding charisms: knowledge, wisdom, and discernment of spirits
- Lifestyle charisms: celibacy, faith, missionary, and voluntary poverty
- Creative charisms: craftsmanship, music, and writing[9]

There are so many other gifts God gives us. And, once we understand that everything we have is a gift from God, we start to see things differently.

Understanding Yourself and Identifying Your Gifts

There are many resources available, for free and for purchase, to help you better understand yourself and your gifts. Common tools used in the workplace include the Big 5 Personality Test, the popular but controversial Myers-Briggs Type Indicator, and the CliftonStrengths Assessment.

Popular Catholic resources include a Catholic version of the CliftonStrengths Assessment, the book *The Temperament God Gave You* (by Art and Laraine Bennett), and the Called & Gifted Discernment Process from the Catherine of Siena Institute. While not specifically a Catholic resource, the 6 Types of Working Genius model was created by Patrick Lencioni, a Catholic management expert. Similarly, the MCode Assessment, which helps users understand their motivations ("M" is for "motivation"), was created by Dr. Joshua Miller, a Catholic philosophy professor at Franciscan University of Steubenville. SENT Ventures also has a resource for decision-making under pressure, inspired by St. Frances Cabrini, available online.

It's important to remember when doing any self-assessment that the results are neither the full truth about you nor a prescription. Use them as a tool to grow in your understanding of yourself and your relationship with God and other people—not as a way to define yourself or put yourself into a box.

Exercising Your Discernment Muscle

Because discernment is, first and foremost, grounded in prayer, becoming good at discernment requires prayer. You can't recognize God's voice if you don't have a relationship with him. Read scripture to get to know him better—dive into the gospels in particular, both to hear Jesus's voice and to learn what he teaches us about the Father and the Holy Spirit. Create a regular prayer routine, even if it's just a couple of minutes each day to start with. (We'll talk more about prayer in chapter 5.)

There are many ways to improve your discernment skills. One approach, based on advice from both Therese Huston and Stacey Sumereau (host of *Called and Caffeinated*),[10] is to imagine what your life will look like if you make a certain choice.

Let's say you've made a particular decision. What is your life like? How did this decision impact it? Do you feel peace about it? For example, let's say you're considering applying for a new position at your company—one that would involve more responsibility (and more pay). Consider what it would be like to be in that position. Do you find the job responsibilities rewarding? Are they achievable (with some coaching and on-the-job learning, perhaps)? Do they take up more of your time—and are you OK with that? Is the new job a good use of your gifts? Is it moving you closer to your longer-term career goals? Is it helping you pay your bills and maybe even give back to the community? Most importantly, do you believe that it is in alignment with God's plan for you?

If you don't know the answers to these questions, take it to prayer. Talk to a mentor or a loved one—someone who knows you well and can coach you through this discernment process. Consider journaling about it as well.

Even during her long dark night of the soul, which spanned almost fifty years, there were ways for Mother Teresa to discern God's will. She still spent time in prayer, even though she couldn't feel his presence. She still had access to the sacraments and scripture. She had her spiritual director. These are all things that we, too, can avail ourselves of in the often-challenging process of discernment. St. Teresa's story can inspire us to surrender our own will to that of the Lord's, whether we're in—or seeking—his light.

St. Teresa of Kolkata: Listening in the Dark

Agnes Gonxha Bojaxhiu felt the call to religious life at age seventeen and joined the Sisters of Loreto, a missionary order, shortly thereafter. She chose the name Sr. Teresa, after St. Thérèse of Lisieux, and served as a teacher and principal of a girls' high school in Calcutta (now Kolkata), India, for eighteen years. While on a train ride to Darjeeling, she heard God's voice giving her what she would later describe as a "call within a call."

The Lord asked Mother Teresa to leave the Sisters of Loreto and begin a new religious community to live with and serve "the poorest of the poor." Mother Teresa spent some time fighting her new call, asking the voice to find someone else to accomplish this mission.[11] Eventually, though, she could no longer say no. With the Vatican's permission, she officially started the Missionaries of Charity in 1950.[12]

Mother Teresa didn't always hear God's voice so clearly. After her death, the world learned from her letters that she experienced a long, painful "dark night of the soul," in which she no longer felt God's presence and didn't hear his voice like she did when he called her to start the Missionaries of Charity.

"Where I try to raise my thoughts to heaven," she wrote to her spiritual director, "there is such convicting emptiness that those very thoughts return like sharp knives and hurt my very soul. . . . I am told God

> lives in me—and yet the reality of darkness and coldness and emptiness is so great that nothing touches my soul."[13]
>
> We may not all experience a dark night to the extent that Mother Teresa did, but we will all experience ebbs and flows in our spiritual life. We are called to remain faithful no matter what we feel when we pray. Mother Teresa did just that. She came to understand, with the help of spiritual direction, that her spiritual darkness was part of her mission: she suffered in order to suffer with Jesus on the Cross and to join the poorest of the poor in their suffering.[14] Despite the amount of time she spent serving the poor, she also spent hours in prayer and adoration, which she said was necessary in order to devote herself to her work.
>
> Mother Teresa's total surrender to Jesus "allowed him to manifest through her his love for each individual. It was the light and love of Jesus himself that radiated from her—in the midst of her own darkness—and that had such an impact on others."[15]

Regardless of whether you use a formal discernment approach or decision-making tool, the most important thing to remember is that God has to be part of the process. Start small; practice praying through your smaller decisions, so that asking the Lord for guidance becomes a habit when you need to make more important decisions.

The next step is surrender. Properly ordered, our lives do not belong to us; they belong to God. The same is true of our career. When asked by a journalist if she had any "special qualities," Mother Teresa responded, "I don't think so. I don't claim anything of the work. It is his work. I am like a little pencil in his hand. That is all. He does the thinking. He does the writing. The pencil has nothing to do with it. The pencil has only to be allowed to be used."[16]

A powerful prayer to help with surrendering to God is the Surrender Novena. Written by Fr. Dolindo Ruotolo, whose cause for canonization has been opened, this novena consists of words that he said came from Jesus and the repetition of the prayer, "O Jesus, I surrender myself to You, take care of everything!" I (Taryn) have prayed the full novena before but sometimes pray just that line in times of distress. It is both a reminder to myself that everything is in Jesus's hands and a plea to Jesus to "take care of everything."

Difficulty and Freedom in Receptivity

The idea of receptivity has always been a challenging one for me (Elise) to swallow. Growing up as a girl in the 90s, I was told I could be anything I wanted to be and do anything boys did. Independence was touted as the supreme value for girls: don't rely on anyone for your own financial independence or happiness.

The reality is, receptivity requires trust and transformation—trust in God and transformation within ourselves. To become the woman I know I'm called to be, I cannot remain static. And neither can you. As we've discussed in this chapter, the first step in making a change in your career is receiving God: his peace, his joy, and his understanding. It is in him that we find ourselves.

The world is loud, perhaps more now than ever before. Even when we are alone, the rest of the world is just a tap of the phone away. So many voices, from the people we know "in real life" to the people we see online, tell us what we should do and who we should be. We know that the most important voice is God's, but it's hard to listen when his voice seems so much quieter than all the others. It takes deliberate practice.

"Receptivity, and in particular feminine receptivity, is the highest expression of cooperation with God," writes Elizabeth M. Kelly in her book *Jesus Approaches*.[17] He has a plan for each of us—a plan that includes our career—and he will give us all the grace we need to accomplish that plan. But that grace won't do us much good if we don't receive and cooperate with it.

It can be scary, but with his grace, we can have the audacity to make the Blessed Mother Mary's words our own and say to God, "Let it be to me according to your word" (Lk 1:38).

Questions for Reflection and Discussion

1. What major decisions have you discerned in your life and career? Did you ask God to guide your discernment?
2. Have you ever heard God's voice, literally or in another way? What did he ask of you? What was the result?
3. Are you discerning a career decision right now? How can you invite God into the discernment process?
4. What gifts or charisms has God given you? How can you be a good steward of those gifts in your work?
5. What difficulties do you have in surrendering your career to God? What can you do to remind yourself that he is in charge?

THREE

IS IT OK TO BUILD WEALTH?

> About the most powerful thing you can do to help a society and economy is get more money in the hands of women.[1]
>
> Sallie Krawcheck, CEO of Ellevest

One of the most frequently asked questions we hear at Catholic Women in Business is, "Is it OK for me to build wealth?" In our experience, many Catholic women frequently feel uncomfortable charging what their work is worth, investing money with the goal of making more money, or negotiating for a higher salary.

It makes sense. After all, the majority of our most well-known saints are religious who literally took vows of poverty. Yet not everyone is called to the religious life—and while everyone is called to be "poor in spirit" (Mt 5:3), spiritual poverty does not necessarily require financial poverty. Spiritual poverty means relying on God for everything, loving him more than money, and trusting him rather than trusting our budget. Scripture says that the love of money (not money itself) is the root of all evil (1 Tm 6:10).

In fact, scripture tells us that wealthy women helped fund Jesus's ministry. As Jesus traveled, he was accompanied not only by the twelve apostles but also by Mary Magdalene; Joanna, the wife of Herod's steward Chuza; Susanna; and others who contributed to his mission (Lk

8:1–3). Their wealth wasn't sinful—far from it; these women were able to use their wealth to help Jesus proclaim the Good News.

Edith Stein wrote that when she converted to Catholicism, she believed that "leading a religious life meant giving up all earthly things and having one's mind fixed on divine things only," but she slowly learned that God has other expectations of us. "I even believe that the deeper someone is drawn to God, the more he has to 'get beyond himself' in this sense, that is, go into the world and carry divine life into it." Even when Edith entered the convent and gave up her earthly belongings, she carried on with some of her philosophical work, adding to the "earthly" gift she left to the world in the form of her talks and writings, which truly carry divine life into it.[2]

We hear so much about the saints who lived beautiful lives of poverty that we can sometimes think that wealth is a barrier to holiness. And, indeed, as Jesus says in the gospels, wealth can make it difficult to become a saint, because it can create a temptation to rely on money instead of on God. However, in Proverbs' famous portrait of the "woman of worth," we read about a woman who works for "profit" and "reaches out her hand to the poor, and extends her arms to the needy" (Prv 31). These verses are not contradictions; Jesus specifies that while it is impossible for a rich man to enter the kingdom of heaven, it is not impossible for him to do so *with God*.

Isn't Money the Root of All Evil?

Elise

I grew up in an upper-middle class household with an entrepreneur father and a stay-at-home mother. Throughout my childhood, my father was building a law firm. As I worked in the office, I saw him take sales calls, meet with clients, and train employees. I was grateful to grow up in a safe and loving household with parents who provided so many resources for me, including a Catholic education. They worked extremely hard to provide me and my siblings opportunities that were never available to them.

Somewhere around my late high school or early college years, a new belief settled into my heart. That idea was that "good" Catholics do not

As Catholics, how do we discern what the Lord is calling our family to regarding work and finances?

For my family, work and income have looked vastly different over time. For the first four years of our marriage, I was working as an entrepreneur and was the main breadwinner for our household while my husband was working full time as a Catholic high school theology teacher and a part-time law student. When we had our first baby, I down shifted my schedule to part-time work at home, and my husband Hunter worked full time. For six months after the birth of our second baby, I was a full-time stay-at-home mom. Now, we are both working full time outside of the home. Throughout all of these changes, the Lord has made it clear to me in prayer that each stage of my career is just that: a stage. Work and our finances are going to continue to change as our family needs change.

In her article "Is It OK to Build Wealth as a Catholic?" Erica Mathews, CFP, notes:

> To provide for the people in our care, we need resources, and it is our responsibility to earn those resources in an ethical manner and build them as God allows. We must not be like the man in the parable who builds a second barn so that he will never have to work again. Rather, we must be like the steward who takes five talents and earns five more so he can return them to the master. If you are building your wealth to return it to the Master in any way he asks, you are being a faithful steward.[3]

Money is a resource that we need to provide for our families and communities. The use of money requires prudence, fortitude, and temperance. When thinking about money, I often think of the scriptural phrase "To whom much is given, of him will much be required" (Lk 12:48). No matter where you are in your financial journey, whatever the Lord has given you up until now is a testament to his provision. Creating and working on financial goals with the Lord's input and guidance is key to our success.

St. Jane Frances de Chantal was a steward of her financial blessings and possessed a keen awareness of the importance of respecting the nature of individuals on her path to sanctity.

St. Jane Frances de Chantal: Sanctity without Poverty or Austerity

Born in 1572, St. Jane Frances de Chantal was a French noblewoman educated, in preparation for marriage, in the Catholic faith, current events, finance, and legal matters. She married a baron and put her education and privileged background to good use by managing his estates while he was on military campaigns. Jane and her husband had four children and were happily married. When the baron was home, they entertained frequently. Sadly, he died at age twenty-eight in a hunting accident.

Grief-stricken, Jane dedicated herself to God in the same way she'd dedicated herself to her husband. She gave away her jewels and created a new rule of life for herself, spending all of her time caring for and educating her children, praying, and doing works of mercy. She even established a hospital dispensary in the attic to serve the sick.

Her father-in-law treated Jane terribly and threatened to disinherit her children if they didn't move in with him, his mistress, and their five children. To protect her children's inheritance, she and her children lived with them for seven years, forbearing the bad treatment with kindness and humility.

In 1604, Jane attended a Lenten sermon by the visiting Bishop (now Saint) Francis de Sales. When he saw her in one of the front rows, he recognized her as a woman he'd seen in a vision in which God told him he'd found a religious congregation with her. Jane had likewise seen Francis in a vision soon after her husband's death. A voice had told her, "This is the man beloved of God and among men into whose hands you are to commit your conscience."[4]

Francis became Jane's spiritual director, and many of their letters to each other survive. He helped her with her perfectionism and counseled her to remain with her children rather than entering religious life. Later, they began the Visitation Order, which had eighty houses by the time Jane died. They wanted the Visitation Order to be a new type of religious congregation for older women and women who were unable to practice the austerities required of other orders—showing that there is a path to sanctity for everyone.

Getting Comfortable with Money

Elise

The subject of money can be fraught with emotion. We all have a history with money. Some of us come from families where money was wielded as a weapon. For others, it was not really a thought. For still others, it was a daily worry.

Over the years of growing businesses, I have had my bank account overdrawn more times than I'd like to admit; I've also become very grateful and proud of how I've been able to provide financially for my family. As an entrepreneur running a marketing agency with employees who depended on salaries generated from our sales, I also had to get comfortable very quickly with bringing up the topic of money with clients. At first, I was very timid and it felt awkward when I would send invoices, even though I was proud of the work I had produced for the client. Truly believing in the value you are providing to a client or an employer is absolutely key to a healthy relationship with money. Whether you are currently happy with your income or not, approaching your finances with a sense of gratitude and dignity sets the tone for how you move forward.

Taryn

I was very timid in my first job out of school. I didn't negotiate my starting salary; in fact, it didn't even occur to me to do so. I graduated in 2010; the economy was still reeling from the 2008 recession, and I was grateful to have any job. I was also a socially anxious, confrontation-averse twenty-one-year-old who didn't know how to stand up for myself or be confident in my abilities. It's not like I'd really had the opportunity to prove myself anywhere other than school, anyway.

Fortunately, I had a wonderful boss who gave me positive feedback as well as correctional advice. She was a fierce advocate for her all-female team, and I'll always be grateful that she was my first supervisor after school. I learned a lot there.

Years later, I was at a different company, where I'd been working as an editor for a couple of years. I'd switched positions once, from a hybrid marketing and editorial role to one focused on editing and managing content. I felt that I deserved a new title, as my responsibilities had increased. So, I told my boss I felt that rather than "editor," my new title should be "assistant editorial director."

Not only did he agree that I needed a new title, but also he told me I needed one that didn't have the word "assistant" in it. I ended up with the title "managing director, digital content."

I'd come a long way.

That first boss frequently recommended the book *Women Don't Ask: The High Cost of Avoiding Negotiation—and Positive Strategies for*

Change (2007). Coauthored by economist Linda Babcock and writer Sara Laschever, the groundbreaking book began a conversation that is still needed in many circles today. It revealed that women are less likely to ask for raises and promotions and offered strategies to help us change that unfortunate truth.

Gaining Confidence to Ask for What Your Work Is Worth

For many years, the narrative was the same: women didn't ask for promotions or raises, so they didn't receive them. But the story is changing. For one thing, more leaders are speaking out about the obstacles that women face in the workplace that might keep them from asking, such as the different expectations many managers have of the two sexes, which can play an important role in whether women are paid what they deserve. More recent research suggests that it is no longer simply a matter of confidence—that women *do* ask for raises, even more than men do. However, we're still less likely to receive them.[5] It's not always that women need to "lean in"; sometimes, it's the organization that needs to pull us up.

As we work for more just workplaces, there are still ways that women can ask for what we want at work.

Consider what else you might be able to negotiate. Research has shown that men and women negotiate equally—but the things they're negotiating can differ. Men are more likely to negotiate for a higher salary, while women are more likely to negotiate for family-friendly work practices.[6]

Come to the negotiation table prepared with data that supports your argument. Use websites like Glassdoor to find out what the market rate is for someone with your experience and title. Gather data about your past performance and demonstrate the value you've provided the company. And, remember your strengths. Draw on your emotional intelligence to understand and manage your own feelings about the negotiation and connect better with your boss.

If you're an entrepreneur, establish pricing for your products or services that reflects your worth. In some ways, setting prices can be even more nerve-racking. But, remember your mission: Who is it that you're serving with your business? Why are you offering the products or services you offer? Who benefits from the money you make? For some tips in this area, see the article "Pricing Your Services as a Freelancer" at Catholic-WomeninBusiness.com.[7]

In the next section, we will take a broader look at this question, to consider how the money we earn on the job benefits not only our families but the wider community as well. This is important to keep in mind as we discern the work to which we have been called—and the responsibility we have before God in managing our finances. This is the lesson that Lisa Canning learned while pursuing her ambitions.

Lisa Canning: Building a Catholic Economy

Lisa Canning began her career as an interior designer, working behind and in front of the camera for HGTV. After her first four babies were born, each eighteen months apart, she was exhausted and unhappy. She made some changes that helped her feel more rested and happier, and people—moms in particular—started asking her what she was doing differently. Those conversations led to her book, *The Possibility Mom*, and her coaching business. In 2023, she also took on the role of president at Guiding Star Project, a national network of life-affirming health care centers.

Lisa said she's always been entrepreneurial and found the idea of making money "like a fun hobby" and "a really good challenge," but when she started listening to outside voices, she would sometimes doubt whether she was meant to earn money as a Catholic wife and mother.

"A Catholic woman should be asking, 'How is my function of working or making money going to impact my family?'" Lisa said. Finding the answer to this question takes discernment—both solo prayer and prayer and conversation with your husband—and the "docility" to follow God's plan, even if it's not what you originally had in mind. "We hold things with loose hands," she said of herself and her husband.

Lisa shared that at the Guiding Star Project, one of the team's core values is "joyfully sacrificial and also faithfully resourceful," and she thinks it's a good way of looking at financial discernment. "It's stepping out in faith and trusting that the Lord will provide, but also using my faculties of reason, of wisdom, of knowledge to make informed decisions."

As a coach—and someone who's benefited from therapy—Lisa said that one of the challenges in letting go of the desire for security and money in particular is that many women have deeply ingrained thought patterns about those topics. These struggles can affect money management as well as generosity. "For me," Lisa said, "giving comes down to building a Catholic economy" by, for instance, supporting Catholic education. Lisa is also known by many Catholic businesswomen as an encouraging and supportive voice in the female Catholic economy in particular.

Lisa concluded by saying, "You are going to have to let the Lord into this dream, and he's going to stretch you. But this stretching is where your true capacity, where your true ability, and where ultimately your sanctity is going to happen."

How Women Share Wealth

In *Letter to Women*, Pope St. John Paul II wrote, "I would like to express particular appreciation to those women who are involved in the various *areas of education* extending well beyond the family: nurseries, schools, universities, social service agencies, parishes, associations and movements. Wherever the work of education is called for, we can note that women are ever ready and willing to give themselves generously to others, especially in serving the weakest and most defenseless" (9).

As of 2014, 59 to 82 percent of the nonprofit workforce was female,[8] and as of 2008, about 85 percent of roles in the Catholic Church that do not require ordination were held by women.[9] Why is that? Are we drawn to these service roles because of our generous hearts?

Research by the Women's Philanthropy Institute (WPI) at Indiana University suggests that the answer might be "yes." Researchers there have found that women are more likely to give than men (there is some evidence to indicate that this pattern holds true in religious giving as well[10]), and women's philanthropy is more likely to be motivated by empathy than men's, which is more likely to be motivated by self-interest.[11] Women also tend to give for personal reasons (i.e., they identify personally with the goals or mission of an organization).[12] While most couples make joint giving decisions, when one person makes the household philanthropy decisions, it's more often the woman.[13] The WPI has also found that many wealthy women feel conflicted about their wealth, echoing what we see in the Catholic Women in Business Facebook group.[14]

We share these statistics not to tear down men—far from it!—but to empower you. Making money can be a good thing, because you can help build God's kingdom with it.

For decades, women ran civil society. Mothers and housewives volunteered at schools, led nonprofit fundraisers, and served on community boards. Now, more women work full time—but those community organizations still need both donors and leaders. Women are coming out of the philanthropic woodwork, giving more publicly[15] and setting an example for both high-dollar and smaller donations. And, because women and men give differently, it's important that both sexes are involved in philanthropy. Here are just two examples of how women make a difference today.

Women are more likely to support organizations that focus on reproductive issues—both pro-life and pro-choice. Women are especially likely to support pro-choice reproductive health organizations,[16] and Catholic women can use their resources to provide an alternative that embraces pro-woman, pro-life health care. For example, the nonprofit FAbM Base, founded by two Catholic women, provides resources on fertility awareness methods of family planning and restorative reproductive medical care. The Guiding Star Project, also founded by a Catholic woman (whom you'll meet in chapter 7), offers pro-life fertility planning and pregnancy, childbirth, postpartum, and family life services in locations across the United States. And, the major pro-life organizations in the United States are led by women.[17]

Women frequently pool their resources in giving circles, selecting organizations to support as a group. In fact, the majority of participants in giving circles are women.[18] Again, this is an area where Catholic women can make an impact, creating Catholic giving circles that select organizations to support that care for people in need and make a difference in the community in ways that are aligned with Catholic values.

Tithing: What Does God Ask of Us for His Church?

St. Paul tells us that "God loves a cheerful giver" (2 Cor 9:7). By giving joyfully, we are sharing God's love with our neighbors and with his Church, not just checking a box. St. Paul also promises us that God will always give abundantly to us (2 Cor 9:8). This promise isn't some prosperity gospel that tells us we will be rich if we are good. Rather, it is a promise that God will give us what we *need*, if not what we *want*. And we can show our trust in God's providence by offering to his Church what is, ultimately, his. Giving not just our money but also our time and talent supports the work of his Bride.

Christians often talk about "tithing," or giving 10 percent of what you earn to the Church. This requirement was established by God in the Old Testament (Lv 27:32). However, the Catholic Church teaches that God does not require us to give a specific amount or percentage to the Church. We are required to "provide for the material needs of the Church . . . each according to his own abilities" (*CCC* 2043). If giving 10 percent of your income is going to impede your ability to provide for yourself or your family, you are not required to give that amount. On the other hand, if you are able to give more than 10 percent, you should do so. As with so many things, the Church provides guidance and leaves the specifics up to our prayerful discernment.

Manage Your Money Mindset

There are a few mindset traps that are all too easy to fall into when it comes to money. One, which we just mentioned, is the prosperity gospel—the idea that God rewards faithful Christians with happiness and wealth. Even if we don't consciously believe this idea is true, it's easy to feel like we "deserve better" when we come on hard times (financial or otherwise). God doesn't promise wealth or happiness in this life; what he does promise us is that he will never leave us (Mt 11:28–30, Mt 28:20) and that he will always give us what we need in order to do what he has called us to do (Lk 12:22–31, Mt 6:25–34, 2 Cor 9:8).

On the other side of the spectrum, we have the scarcity mindset. As personal finance journalist Katie Gatti Tassin writes, "Scarcity mindset is the white-knuckle grip that tells you if you let go for *even a second*, everything will disappear—that you've built a precarious house of cards that you need to relentlessly guard."[19] Tassin does not write from a Catholic perspective (although she says she went to a Catholic elementary school), but she acknowledges that there's a certain amount of letting go and trusting required to have a healthy mindset around money. For Catholics, that trust should be in God. While we should manage and plan our finances prudently, we should do so with a loose grip, knowing that ultimately he is in control.

Taryn

I have swung in two different directions in terms of my money mindset over the years. For much of my twenties, money caused a lot of anxiety, and I avoided thinking about it as much as I could. This avoidance resulted in living paycheck to paycheck, occasionally overdrawing on my bank account, and racking up credit card debt. I didn't earn a lot of money, and I didn't have the fortitude to create and stick to a budget. By the grace of God and with the advice of my now-husband, I was able to pay off my credit cards and get my finances under control before our wedding. Creating and maintaining a budget was a new and difficult experience for me, and I had to learn to be temperate in my spending (particularly when it came to buying books, my most frequent temptation!).

Because of this history, I now sometimes veer toward the other direction and can be afraid to spend money. My husband sometimes reminds me, "Money is a tool." It's not good or bad in itself, and neither is using it. We certainly want to be prudent in how we steward the money we earn, and it's OK to use it to purchase necessities, support the philanthropic causes we care about (including, always, our parish), and even purchase some luxuries for our family. I've been able to find a balance in saving for the future, relying on God rather than our paycheck, and discerning the best use of our finances with my husband.

Do Not Be Afraid

When it comes to money, we must remember the principal reasons for building a business: to pursue our most basic human needs, our holiness, and our excellence. St. John Paul II addressed this principle in his encyclical *Centesimus Annus* (*The Hundredth Year*): "The purpose of a business firm is not simply to make a profit, but is to be found in its very existence as a community of persons who in various ways are endeavoring to satisfy their basic needs, and who form a particular group at the service of the whole of society" (35).

As Catholic women in business, we cannot be afraid or overly possessive of money. In Aristotle's *Nicomachean Ethics*, he defines virtue as the "mean" or "middle ground" between habits of acting. It's easy to operate out of fear when it comes to money. We can overspend or we can be miserly. We can go weeks without looking at our bank accounts or we can be overly rigorous, checking on it every hour.

We cannot define for you what a balanced approach to money looks like in your own life, but we can encourage you to trust your instincts and in your ability (in partnership with your husband if you are married) to discern the Lord's will for your finances. Just remember, your worth goes well beyond your income. Money is a tool in your toolbox as a Catholic woman in business. Meghan Maloof Berdellans illustrates for us how to wield it wisely.

Meghan Maloof Berdellans: Holy Spirit–Led Discernment in Work and Money

Meghan Maloof Berdellans is a real estate executive, digital marketing consultant, and philanthropist in Miami, Florida. In 2015, she managed the Archdiocese of New York's social media for Pope Francis's visit.

Later, she said, "When I was making the most money I'd ever made was actually when I didn't feel like I was making enough." She worked through this mindset with her therapist, and one day at Mass, she heard a message in prayer: "The Lord gave, and the Lord has taken away; blessed be the name of the Lord" (Jb 1:21).

On the other hand, Meghan has never questioned whether it was OK to earn money and build wealth. She partially credits this confidence to her uncle, who was president of Avon and a mentor of hers. She's frequently asked, though, if it can be moral to build wealth as a Catholic woman.

"I think society has placed a heavy stressor on women to really pour too much of themselves and think of others before they think of themselves," Meghan said. While there's virtue, of course, in thinking of others before yourself, she believes that there is pressure on women to do so at the expense of themselves. "If God is instilling a purpose into the wife and it creates an income, there's nothing wrong with that," she said.

To make sure she's putting God at the center of her money-making and financial planning, Meghan prays throughout the day, from her morning Rosary to nightly prayers with her husband. The result of praying without ceasing (1 Thes 5:17) is, for Meghan, a valuable part of her discernment toolbox. "I've felt the Holy Spirit working through me in business throughout the day," she said, "even in business decisions that I've had to make. . . . [As] much money as I have or as little money as I have, as long as I put him first, everything's gonna be OK."

Meghan sees volunteering and philanthropy as an important part of her work. For women wanting to take the first steps in giving back, her advice is to find something you're passionate about that has a community around it. For instance, she is one of the leaders and supporters of the Endometriosis Coalition due to her own experience with the illness.

Questions for Reflection and Discussion

1. When you think about money, what emotions come up? How do they affect how you manage your finances?
2. Are you earning a just wage based on your skills, time, and education? Should you negotiate with your employer or your customers for a higher income? (Or, if you make more than what the market would consider just, perhaps you can consider giving more away?)
3. What anxieties, if any, come up when it comes to negotiating? How can you build your confidence in this key skill?
4. Do you currently give money to your parish or any other philanthropic cause? How can you determine an amount—even a small one—to give, at least to your parish, monthly or annually?

FOUR

HOW DO I BUILD STRONG RELATIONSHIPS AT WORK?

> I want to "rebrand" the idea of a "nice girl" as someone who is not meek or a people pleaser, but who uses her authentic kindness to sidestep regressive stereotypes about what a strong leader looks like.[1]
>
> Fran Hauser, *The Myth of the Nice Girl*

Taryn

Relationships have always been challenging for me, as someone with social anxiety. It can take me a long time to feel comfortable talking to someone new, even about the most mundane of topics. Once I'm comfortable, I'm a total chatterbox—and don't hesitate to share my often strong opinions.

There was a sales director I used to clash with over client projects. As the creative (the writer), I always wanted what would make for the best copy or the best content. She frequently advocated for my opinions with clients, but sometimes, they were insistent on their own visions. She'd come back to me and tell me I had to do it the clients' way, and I never liked to hear that. I had to learn that it was a balancing act—I could offer my expert opinion, but I had to have the humility to (within reason) do what clients wanted. At the end of the day, it was their project, not mine.

You'd think that this sales director and I wouldn't want to hang out much outside of collaborating on these projects. It was quite the contrary, though. She was one of my closest friends in this job. We frequently had lunch together, and I'd been to her house. We still keep in touch, even though we don't have the convenience of being able to shout at each other from our desks.

Why did we get along so well, even though we so often disagreed while working together? It was because we'd built our relationship on trust and respect. We admired each other as professionals, knew that the other person was great at her job, and got to know each other on a more personal level. By the end of my time at this company, she was inviting me to a lot of client meetings so I could talk with our clients face-to-face, and I learned a lot from her about communication and sales—skills that I use now as co-president of Catholic Women in Business.

This relationship would not have been possible without humility, which I often learned the hard way through embarrassing mistakes, and empathy. These two skills are key to building relationships at work (and outside of it—just ask any spouse how well their marriage would go without humility and empathy!).

Elise

I was horribly bullied in middle school. It's taken a lot of time and therapy to address the wounds that those experiences burrowed into my heart. Because of this, female relationships haven't come naturally to me. It took me a long time to build trust and feel at ease in friendships. Eventually, as I grew into young adulthood, I slowly made lasting female friendships that have weathered many a storm.

I know I'm not alone in the experience of struggling with other female relationships. Place an already possibly difficult relationship in a stressful environment such as the workplace, and you have a recipe for complications. Whether you work with mostly men or mostly women or work in an industry that has an equal mix of both, cultivating professional relationships takes emotional investment. Having been an employee, founder, and executive in several companies over the past ten years, I've learned how to operate within relationships as a peer and as a leader. Both types of relationships require different skills and discernment processes.

As we explore the dynamics of work relationships in the following chapter, we hope to encourage you to invest the time and energy in the people the Lord has placed in your life through your work community. Amid deadlines, projects, and proposals, the Lord never wastes an opportunity for you to receive and show his love through the people in your life, even your work colleagues.

Made for Community

There's no job that doesn't require working with other people. Therefore, there's no job that doesn't involve relationships.

We were made to be in community. "It is not good that the man should be alone," God said (Gn 2:18), and "man" includes "woman," too. While romantic relationships, family relationships, and friendships will likely be the closest, most important relationships we have, our relationships with our colleagues, employees, customers, and supervisors are important as well. Positive relationships at work improve our well-being and are an opportunity for us to serve and evangelize.

Both in and out of the workplace, the intuitive gifts of women tend to give us an edge in the "soft skills" of relationship-building—and this knowledge can be empowering. Edith Stein wrote that the feminine soul is "fashioned to be a shelter in which other souls may unfold,"[2] and research shows that women tend to be more other-focused and emotionally connected with people than men are.[3]

How can we embrace and cultivate our ability to relate with others? It starts with humility.

Receive in Humility

Humility is often equated with groveling and with thinking poorly of yourself. But humility isn't self-punishment; it's self-awareness. As St. Teresa of Ávila wrote, "Humility is the truth."[4] She went on to say it is a basic truth that by ourselves, we are nothing (Phil 4:13). It's not enough to have the awareness of your strengths and weaknesses—true humility includes knowing that your strengths are gifts from God, being grateful for those gifts, and having the courage to use them in service to him. It also includes the knowledge that your faults are things that (only with God's grace) you must work to overcome by growing in virtue.

Humility is essential in cultivating authentic Christian relationships. Knowing your limitations and your strengths means you can make a true offering of yourself to the other person. Relying on God to help you be a good friend or colleague, rather than just yourself, means that you have the Holy Spirit to help you. (Plus, no one wants to be in a relationship with an arrogant, prideful person!)

Humility is foundational to the Christian life, but business experts are also coming to see the practical benefits of this virtue. Jim Collins, author of the business classics *Good to Great* and *Built to Last*, found in his research that the most effective leaders not only have strong wills but also demonstrate great humility.[5] As Dr. Ryne Sherman notes, one of the reasons humble leaders are so effective is because they are willing to ask for help and receive feedback (also two essential elements of a strong friendship).[6] In other words, you can't be successful without the humility to find out how to improve.

Humility is required for receptivity, because you have to be aware of a lack in order to receive. To receive God, you have to acknowledge your total dependence on him. And to receive the people he has put in your life, you have to acknowledge that they have a lot to give you, too.

Earlier in my (Taryn's) career, I didn't like to ask too many questions. I'd always been seen as the smart one—which I thought meant that I had to have all the answers. (It also probably did not help when making friends; it's hard to get close to someone who never has questions or needs help.) And there's certainly something to be said about trying to solve problems on your own, but I've learned that there is something beautiful about having the humility to admit when you need help and to accept that help. (Many of us learn this lesson as new mothers when our friends set up a meal train for us!)

In this way, our feminine receptivity can be a huge boon to our work—and, in fact, Huston's investigation of decision-making found that women are more likely to seek feedback when making decisions! If we are by nature more receptive, more humble, then we can build relationships of mutual support—not a "you scratch my back, I scratch yours" quid pro quo but supportive, loving collaboration. Humble receptivity builds mutual trust, and with that trust in place, working relationships have the capability of creating powerful results for the business and the people it serves.

Demonstrate Empathy and Compassion

Scripture tells us to "rejoice with those who rejoice, weep with those who weep" (Rom 12:15). Doing so requires empathy. While we tend to think of empathy in terms of our closest personal relationships, it's also important in our relationships with colleagues and clients. After all, we've all likely seen what happens when there's a lack of empathy in the workplace, whether in our own experience or in the news.

There are two types of empathy: emotional and cognitive. Emotional empathy is feeling what another person feels and responding emotionally. Cognitive empathy enables us to take the step of processing that emotion and using it to help us understand the other person and their thoughts and behaviors. The good news for us is that women tend to be better at both kinds of empathy than men.[7]

Taryn

For many women, the challenge isn't being more empathetic—it's balancing empathy with assertiveness and boundaries. For example, I tend to be a people-pleaser. I don't like to say "no" to requests, and I hate feeling like I've let someone down. I also tend to take on too much of other people's pain—to the point where I'm not helpful and it's stealing my peace. It's taken practice (and that practice is ongoing!) to learn to set boundaries with people. When I overcommit myself, I end up without enough bandwidth to be able to serve anyone—which, as Fran Hauser points out in *The Myth of the Nice Girl*, isn't actually nice at all.

I've also learned that I sometimes have to shut out news of what's happening to people outside of my sphere of influence. My "doomscrolling" motto has become, "Say a prayer and move on." When I see a social media post or news story about people in pain, I say a prayer for them and then carry on with my day.

Active Listening

We've all experienced the feeling of talking to someone who is not listening to us. Sure, maybe they're looking at us and nodding their head, but they aren't really taking in what we're saying. On the other hand, we've all probably been guilty of this half-listening, too.

Maybe you also know someone who really listens, though—who makes you feel like you are the only thing that matters in that moment. My husband listens like that; it's one of the first things I noticed about him when we met. I've also been blessed with managers who really listened to me when I brought them my concerns and with whom performance reviews were an opportunity for a conversation, not just a box to check for human resources.

Active listening is receptivity plus empathy. It means listening with the purposeful intention of understanding the other person's meaning, including what they are saying as well as what they are communicating nonverbally.[8] We all get distracted sometimes during conversations, but active listening is a skill we can cultivate.

In her book *The Art of Active Listening*, Heather R. Younger provides a model for active listening—a five-step cycle:

1. Recognize the unsaid: Pay attention to both verbal and nonverbal cues.
2. Seek to understand: Be present, curious, and empathetic. Ask questions or repeat what you hear to make sure you understand what the other person is communicating.
3. Decode: Take the time to reflect on what the person tells you before you act on it.
4. Act: Decide how you will respond compassionately.
5. Close the loop: Communicate your plan of action to the other person.[9]

In other words, we'd point out, it's doing exactly what Jesus tells us in the gospels we should do—seeing other people as Jesus in disguise

(Mt 25:45) and listening to them as we would listen to him. Regina Boyd provides a powerful example of how to do so.

Regina Boyd: Managing Relationships and Conflict with Empathy

Regina Boyd is a counselor and author who owns a private practice. Prior to starting her own business, she experienced healthy workplace cultures, where she felt like a welcomed part of a team, and unhealthy workplace cultures, where there was gossip and a lack of boundaries and trust.

In the healthy workplace culture, Regina said, weekly team meetings were the highlight of her week. "Usually people complain about team meetings," she said, but here, "it was an opportunity to connect with each other, give collaborative support on cases that we were working on, or just ask for help [and] celebrate birthdays." Rather than being a waste of time or an opportunity for leaders to flex their authority, these meetings were a true team-building experience, a way for employees to get to know and support each other, and a place where the team built trust.

Regina says she tries to think back to that time today when working with others so she treats them in a similar way. She also stays focused on "the understanding that this other person has something to offer and gifts that I don't have, or will see something from a different angle that I don't see. I want to be open and receptive to that, because that's only going to help make us better."

To that end, Regina says, it's important to her that she always asks for input after she makes a suggestion—and does so in a genuine way, so that other people know she really values their perspective and doesn't think she has all the answers.

Of course, conflict is inevitable—and can be scary, Regina acknowledges. She likes to reframe it "as an opportunity to grow closer to that person, to learn more about them, to connect and understand them on a deeper level."

Ultimately, Jesus tells us to love our neighbor, and "everyone is a neighbor—our coworkers, our subordinates . . . everyone's deserving of respect and working in a non-hostile work environment," Regina says. It starts with "saying hello, learning about people, remembering small details about what's happening with them."

The Dark Side of Empathy: Gossip

Taryn

I never thought I had a problem with gossip. I didn't really talk badly about my friends or coworkers with other friends or coworkers, and I was pretty good at keeping other people's secrets.

Then, one day, I was deep into the weeds of comments on a post in a Facebook group. I didn't know the original poster (OP) or any of the commenters, but I was riveted. I almost commented on it myself. And, suddenly, I realized that I was not immune to gossip. For me, it presented as nosiness. Why did I care about the problems happening in the OP's marriage? Why was I so invested in the drama unfolding in the comments? It had nothing to do with me.

I was horrified. And, since then, I have had to confess nosiness several times, each time shame-faced at my lack of improvement. I've left several Facebook groups to avoid the temptation of scrolling, judging, and commenting. I've resisted asking friends for more details about random women online that they were telling me about. And I've realized that in the fallen world we live in, my empathy has a dark side: being overly invested in other people's problems.

Edith Stein wrote about this tendency—that while women are drawn to other people, we must work toward moderation by being "anchored completely in Jesus." Otherwise, we may become "overly wrapped up" in the people around us. (On the other hand, we can become so wrapped up in our "professional activity" that it causes "infidelity toward [our] feminine vocation.") The answer, she wrote, is total surrender to the Lord.[10]

Mindy Edgington: Loving Even Difficult Coworkers

Mindy Edgington shows how we can bring understanding to our challenging work relationships. Mindy manages an information security risk and compliance team and is passionate about fostering difficult conversations and loving your neighbor, even (or especially) when it's hard.

Mindy has often worked on male-dominated teams, and she said she enjoys and leans into that complementarity. She's had many male coworkers with whom she had excellent relationships where they respected and leveraged each other's strengths. On the other hand, she's had some male coworkers who have exhibited more stereotypically "toxically masculine" behaviors, such as sharing distasteful humor. In scenarios with colleagues of either gender who demonstrate bad behavior in the workplace, Mindy noted, she's learned to try to focus on cultivating virtue in herself so that she can lead by example. When she hears someone gossiping, for instance, she tries to figure out why. If they're gossiping just to gossip, she'll try to steer the conversation in a different direction. If they're gossiping because they're feeling insecure or having a genuine problem, she tries to help solve it with them.

And, on the occasions when Mindy has a conversation that she feels isn't as charitable as it should be, she goes to Confession. "Luckily, we have a very forgiving father who wants us to be better," she said. "I can get back into the saddle of having edifying conversations and leading by a good example."

Mindy is intentional in how she approaches maintaining relationships. She writes in her planner when she hasn't talked to someone in a while to make sure she checks in with them. "That's how I've been able to keep strong relationships," she said, "both professionally and personally."

From there, she makes sure to keep her relationships and conversations authentic. "I believe that we could actually be more productive and have stronger relationships if we were just ourselves," she said. "Now, does that mean you might get burned? Maybe so—that's kind of the risk of being vulnerable—but I think that we're not happy with our current work environment. And I think that we can help it by being ourselves."

Building Community: Networking and Friendships

US Surgeon General Vivek Murthy declared a loneliness epidemic in a *Harvard Business Review* article in 2017[11]—three years before the COVID-19 pandemic exacerbated people's isolation. In 2021, Harvard researchers found that 36 percent of all Americans (and more than half of young adults and mothers of young children) felt "serious loneliness,"[12] and the problem also exists in many other countries worldwide.[13]

This is a problem not just for our mental health but also our physical health, as Surgeon General Murthy recently stated in a general advisory.[14] God did not create us to live life alone—even contemplative religious, who live away from the world, do so in community. Building community is important for our spiritual health, our emotional health, and our career, as the plethora of networking organizations and advice books indicate.

In fact, Catholic Women in Business was created because of a need for community, and we keep the goal of building community front of mind when we plan new offerings for CWIB.

As an extrovert with social anxiety disorder, I tend to be known as "the quiet one" in a new group—until, at some point, I'm not! This was especially true when I worked in an office. I'd join a new team and be timid at first, but eventually, the exposure of working with the same people forty hours a week gave me a certain level of comfort and confidence in talking with them. As a result, I've made good friends in each organization I've worked in—the most recent and best being Elise!

Networking has always been difficult for me, particularly back when it was usually in person. I can still remember one event where I arrived, went inside and got a name tag, and then went back to my car for a panic attack and phone call to my boyfriend (now husband).

Thanks to a great therapist, it's been a while since I've panicked like that, but I still get nervous meeting new people. And you don't have to have diagnosed social anxiety to feel nervous about networking. If you are uncomfortable networking but have to for your job or business—or you simply believe it will be beneficial—there are some mindset shifts you can make that will help.

Remember that you're interacting with children of God. They may seem intimidating, especially if they're further along their career path than you are, but they, like you, are made in his image and likeness. They have struggles, they sin, and they have dreams God's placed on their heart. Keeping this in mind will help make them more approachable—and help avoid feeling like you're simply being transactional.

Enter networking events with the goal of helping someone else. Yes, you have your own objectives in terms of finding customers, looking for a new job opportunity, or meeting a potential mentor. But, if your primary goal is to see what you can offer someone else, you're more likely to make authentic connections that result in mutually beneficial outcomes. If you're like many women, you'll also probably feel more confident making an offer to help than you will asking for something for yourself.

Make it a goal to get to know someone else rather than simply to share about yourself. I've always found other people fascinating; I love reading biographies and memoirs (I even always make sure to read the brief bios at the end of articles in magazines and on blogs). But, I was always so worried about how I would be perceived at a networking event that I forgot how fun it could be to get to know the other people there! What a difference it would have made if I'd gone to networking events prepared with questions in order to get to know other people.

What if You Work Remotely?

Elise and I started working together in 2018 but didn't meet in person until 2023. Elise lives in Maryland, and I live in North Carolina. Despite the distance, we've built a collaborative, trusting relationship using video calls, text messages, and voice memos. It may be easier to build relationships over coffee and office drop-ins, but you can do it virtually, too. It just takes intention.

There's always the possibility of negotiating the situation that best fits your lifestyle and family needs (or lack thereof)—or of finding another job. But, if you're in a remote or partly remote job, here are some strategies we've found helpful in our long-distance business partnership:

Schedule regular check-ins. As busy working wives and mothers, we can easily get caught up from day to day and not check in with each other. We have a standing meeting one evening each week, after the kids are in bed, to check in with each other in a Zoom meeting or FaceTime call. We usually have specific business points we need to cover, but it's also helpful just to see each other's faces and catch up on how we're doing. Talking over everything from the status of a project to our children's milestones helps us keep the business running and our relationship strong.

Take advantage of technology. Everyone's familiar with Zoom now, but there are many other tools we take advantage of to run Catholic Women in Business. We've found that voice memos are a great way to send each other quick, personable messages while taking care of a toddler, cooking dinner, or running into the office or a doctor's appointment. We also use project management software to keep track of meetings and projects and use Google Docs for everything from sharing podcast episodes to writing this book.

Create face time when possible—but also respect people's time. When I took over as managing editor, I (Taryn) immediately decided to schedule video calls every time I onboarded a new writer. I never share any information that can't be shared by email. However, as of this writing, only one writer has ever been local to me, and I appreciate getting to talk "face-to-face" to kick-start our relationship. We also have a quarterly writing team call to brainstorm ideas and get some face time with each other. However, the call is optional, and I rely mostly on Slack messages and email to communicate with the writing team. Keeping this balance of face time and asynchronous communication means that I respect each writer's time (and my own!) while building more personal relationships with them. With a large and growing team spread across four continents now, it's important to me that each writer is more than a name. However, as they're all volunteers at this point with full-time jobs or children, or both, to take care of, it's also important to me that I don't take up too much of their precious time.

Leave the house. Especially if you're an extrovert who thrives being around other people, find places to work outside your house. There are always coffee shops, of course—but public libraries are free! You might meet other people who work remotely, and as you become friends, perhaps you can work together at each other's houses or in the community one or two mornings a week.

Mary and Elizabeth provide an inspiring example of not only a family relationship but also a deep friendship—even though they, too, lived at a distance from each other.

Mary and Elizabeth: Sisterhood, Not Competition

As we reflect on relationships in this chapter, we're reminded of the story of Mary, the mother of Jesus, and Elizabeth, her older cousin.

After telling Mary that she will conceive the Son of God, Gabriel the archangel tells her that Elizabeth, who believed she was barren, had also conceived a son (he would become John the Baptist).

St. Luke tells us that Mary "went with haste" to visit Elizabeth after her visit from Gabriel (Lk 1:39). Why? We can only speculate. Perhaps she sought mentorship from Elizabeth, who was six months ahead of her in terms of motherhood (Lk 1:36) and many years ahead of her in terms of life experience. Perhaps she wanted to help Elizabeth prepare for the birth. Perhaps she wanted to celebrate their miraculous pregnancies together. Perhaps it was all of the above.

When Mary arrived at Elizabeth's house, the Holy Spirit let Elizabeth know that Mary was carrying her Savior by causing John to "[leap] for joy" in her womb (Lk 1:44).

How many of us would have felt resentful in this moment? Elizabeth finally was pregnant—a miraculous child heralded by a visit from an angel. And her younger cousin one-upped her by conceiving the Son of God! Yet, Elizabeth rejoices and humbles herself in the face of "the mother of [her] Lord" (Lk 1:43).

Mary, in turn, rejoices aloud at the blessing of Jesus, both for her and for her people. This prayer is known as the Magnificat and is one of the most celebrated passages in the Bible. Again, Mary doesn't lord it over Elizabeth or try to show how important she is. Instead, she expresses her gratitude to God.

We don't know what happened next, but we can speculate. Maybe Mary stayed for the birth of John the Baptist. Maybe she helped Elizabeth get through those difficult postpartum days or even weeks. Maybe Elizabeth was there when Mary first felt Jesus kick.

How much did their presence help these women through a challenging time? How much did it encourage them to rejoice all the more in their miraculous children? And how can we, as friends, coworkers, managers, mentors, and spiritual mothers, imitate their example?

Better Together: Complementarity

No chapter on building workplace relationships would be complete without talking about men. While our team at Catholic Women in Business is made up of women, we both enjoy collaborating with men (including our husbands!) and believe that in general, it's better when men and women work together.

When God created man, he said, "It is not good that the man should be alone; I will make him a helper fit for him" (Gn 2:18). God then made woman; and man, on seeing her, said, "This at last is bone of my bones and flesh of my flesh" (Gn 2:23).

"Helper" does not mean that man is superior to woman. Rather, as the catechism says, "Man and woman were made 'for each other' . . . [God] created them to be a communion of persons, in which each can be a 'helpmate' to the other, for they are equal as persons ('bone of my bones . . .') and complementary as masculine and feminine" (*CCC* 372). The most obvious example of this complementarity is in marriage, but the masculine and feminine are also complementary when it comes to business.

Companies with greater equity in terms of the representation of both men and women tend to perform better financially, be more innovative, and better meet the needs of their customers (after all, consumer purchases are primarily made by women, and 41 percent of purchases in business-to-business industries are made by women).[15]

Questions for Reflection and Discussion

1. How do you feel when you go to a networking event? How can you reframe the event so that it's something that can be mutually beneficial for you and the people you meet?
2. Are there any areas of your life where you feel that your relationships could be improved? What are three steps you can take today to strengthen your relationships or network?
3. Do you tend to overempathize with other people? If so, how can you find a better balance between compassion and self-care?

4. When you're in a conversation with someone else, how well are you listening to them? What is one step you can take today to improve your active listening skills?

FIVE

HOW DO I KEEP THE FAITH IN A SECULAR WORKPLACE?

> I have given them your word; and the world has hated them because they are not of the world, even as I am not of the world. I do not pray that you should take them out of the world, but that thou should keep them from the evil one. They are not of the world, even as I am not of the world. Sanctify them in the truth; your word is truth. As you sent me into the world, so I have sent them into the world. And for their sake I consecrate myself, that they also may be consecrated in truth.
>
> John 17:14–19

Elise

Although the Lord eventually called me to use my gifts in a secular environment, initially I found myself drawn to an educational path that focused on my spiritual formation. As I mentioned in chapter 3, I was resistant to the idea of building wealth for its own sake, and so I was planning to graduate with my master's in theological studies and teach or work in Catholic ministry.

Directly after graduating with an undergraduate degree at the Catholic University of America in May 2013, I enrolled in a master's in theology program at the John Paul II Institute in Washington, DC. I attended for one year and absolutely loved my classes and the community I had found. I was studying all of the documents and writings that formed St. John Paul II's teachings around marriage and family. My husband and I got engaged in November, and everything felt perfect.

Then, the following spring, something started to change inside of me. As the weather began warming, the Lord began slowly tugging on my heart in prayer, telling me that something wasn't quite right. For months, I felt like the princess and the pea: No matter how hard I tried to ignore this feeling, it just kept growing.

One morning, while in my apartment alone between classes, I was stopped in my tracks with a moment of clarity that I knew was a gift from the Holy Spirit. As much as I loved studying theology, I realized that I was walking down a path that wasn't where I would thrive. I had always had an interest in public relations and marketing (it was even my major for a semester in college) but hadn't pursued it. After speaking with my parents, discerning with Hunter, and applying to several master's programs in media and journalism, I decided on a twelve-month master's program in communications with a focus on marketing at Johns Hopkins University. I applied, was accepted, dropped out of the Institute, and began a new degree program—all within a few months.

Looking back, I now can see that my twenty-three-year-old self was afraid of working outside the Church and in the secular world. I had experienced a powerful encounter with Christ in college that led to a deeper faith than I had ever known before. I was terrified of losing that relationship and faith.

Could I be a practicing lay Catholic while living and working in the secular world? Could my faith endure outside the confines of working within the Church? Fifteen years later, I'm incredibly grateful to say that the answer is "yes."

Everyday Living as a Catholic in the Secular Workforce

> You are the salt of the earth, but if salt has lost its taste, how shall its saltiness be restored? It is no longer good for anything except to be thrown out and trampled under

> foot by men. You are the light of the world. A city set on a hill cannot be hidden. Nor do men light a lamp and put it under a basket, but on a stand, and it gives light to all in the house. Let your light so shine before men, so that they may see your good works and give glory to your Father who is in heaven.
>
> Matthew 5:13–16

Elise

I've worked in both corporate America and as an entrepreneur, and both environments are challenging as a Catholic. Currently, I work in a high-stress, fast-paced environment where our lawyers are representing people who are at one of the lowest points in their lives. There is a lot at stake, and there is little, if any, downtime.

This is where the Lord has called me in this season of life. It has required more self-knowledge and more trust in the Lord than any other stage in my career thus far. It's easy to get discouraged and lose focus of my "why." It has pushed me to use new skills and leadership abilities that I didn't even know I possessed. So, why did the Lord call me to work in the secular world and not in ministry?

Since that moment of grace in my apartment in spring 2014, I have felt a strong pull to be "salt and light" to the world. My workplace is my field, and each day I am out there surveying the land, pulling up weeds, planting new seeds, and strengthening roots. It's work that requires endurance and patience. The relationships that I'm building in this space, with those of all different faiths and backgrounds, would most likely not have happened in a church setting. Instead, my work is my ministry.

Every day, I offer people simple opportunities to encounter Jesus, especially through my words and actions. Kindness and generosity go a long way in corporate America. As a leader, you have a million things on your plate, and it does take extra effort to remember birthdays, sit and talk with someone instead of rushing to that next meeting, or follow up about an event in someone's life.

Daily Mass and the Rosary have been critical to my ability to undertake my work. With little ones, daily Mass isn't possible every day of the week, but we do strive to attend at least one daily Mass in addition to Sundays. Over the pandemic, I developed a relationship with the Blessed Mother, and it has changed my life. I had struggled with *feeling* close to her in the past, but the more time I spent with her, the more I grew in confidence of her love for me and desire to lead me to Jesus. There are many times that I'm in the middle of a meeting and suddenly am inspired to know what to say next to solve a problem or feel a deep peace, and I know I'm receiving the graces of the Eucharist and the Rosary.

I keep a crucifix visible on my office bookshelf. It's a daily reminder of who I am working for and who is with me in this work. Throughout the day, I will stop to pray before meetings; just ten seconds and a few deep breaths help me to refocus and remind myself that Jesus always walks before me in every situation at work.

These seemingly small tasks have become profoundly meaningful, helping me to stay connected to my faith and God during this busy season of working and family life. As a homemaker (yes, I still identify as a homemaker even though I work outside of the home!), I strive with my husband to create peace and a sense of the eternal in our home through living the liturgical calendar set forth by the Church. We celebrate our family's patron saints, pray the Angelus together before we leave for work, and have a dedicated little oratory, or prayer area, in our living room where we attempt weekly family Rosaries. All of these habits at home pour into our ability to make our work a fruitful ministry rooted in the Lord.

St. Gianna Beretta Molla sets for us a clear example of living out God's plan, to the point of surrendering everything to him.

St. Gianna Beretta Molla: Putting Faith and Family First

Born in Italy in 1922, Gianna Beretta became a pediatrician because of her love of children and pregnant women. She felt that she served God by serving her patients. "'He who visits a sick person, helps me,' Jesus said. . . . Just as the priest can touch Jesus, so do we touch Jesus in the bodies of our patients."[1]

Gianna married Pietro Molla, an engineer. Their letters testify to their great love for God, each other, and their children. During each of her pregnancies, Gianna experienced hyperemesis gravis and other problems. She was hospitalized during her third pregnancy and miscarried her next two babies.[2]

Due to the demands of his career and their growing family, Pietro asked Gianna to give up her medical practice if she became pregnant for a sixth time. She agreed.

During her next pregnancy, doctors found a fibroma (a noncancerous tumor) in her uterus. Some of her colleagues recommended that she have an abortion and remove the fibroid, which would have low risks for her. She could also have the fibroma removed but save the baby's life; this option would be the riskiest for her own health.

Gianna could also have a hysterectomy, which would end the life of her child and prevent her from having any more biological children. Under the Catholic understanding of the principle of double effect, as long as doctors tried to save the child's life after removing the uterus, this choice would have been morally permissible.[3]

Gianna decided to have only the fibroma removed. She told her doctors and Pietro that if given a choice between saving her life or the baby's, they were to save the baby's. At the end of the pregnancy, doctors tried to induce labor but ultimately had to perform a C-section, and she had a healthy baby girl weighing almost ten pounds. Unfortunately, Gianna died soon afterward due to an infection in the lining of her abdomen.[4]

Working in a secular culture and a secular industry, it can be difficult, and even countercultural, to put faith and family first. As we will see in the next chapter, doing so does not always involve leaving the workforce. But, it always means sacrifice. St. Gianna is the perfect role model and intercessor when discerning these types of decisions.

Taryn

I always worked in a secular field until I had my daughter and started focusing my work time on Catholic Women in Business and other Catholic editing and writing. Especially since I've always been in the American South, I got used to being the "token Catholic"—the odd woman out who came to the Valentine's Day office party in 2018 fasting and with ashes on her forehead. (Ash Wednesday fell on Valentine's Day that year.)

That was also the year I started living my faith more openly online. I started my blog *Everyday Roses*, which was inspired by St. Thérèse, at the end of 2017. In early 2018, I went to the North Carolina Right to Life's annual prayer breakfast with some friends. The organizers—perhaps excited to see a group of young adults there—asked us to lead a prayer. I wrote about the experience in a blog post, and one of my coworkers, a vehemently pro-choice woman with a fallen-away Catholic family, told me the next morning, "Your blog might make me Catholic yet, Taryn." She said the blog post had brought her to tears. We've since lost touch, and as far as I know she is still not religious and is still pro-choice. However, it seemed to me that the Holy Spirit used my blog to plant a seed. Who knows what will sprout?

Several years later, I had a similar experience with another coworker, a pro-choice, very secular woman. She had some values that were markedly different from my own, but we also shared views that helped us to work well together. When I told her that I was leaving the company to care for my daughter full time, I expected judgment for becoming a "stay-at-home mom," but I felt none. Instead, she told me that she'd always admired how I'd lived out my values in the workplace and as a volunteer in the community. It was a powerful reminder to me that in a secular, sometimes seemingly anti-Christian world, we can be powerful witnesses of what it really means to be Christian.

At least for now, I believe that God is calling me to work for a Catholic business. After years of working in a secular industry, I treasure my friendships with other Catholics and want to help my daughter cultivate friendships with Catholic children. And yet, I have to steel myself against the temptation to live in a "faith bubble." Sometimes I find myself wanting to control my daughter's social interactions or going out of my way to avoid disagreements about faith or values. These desires come from fear, and we are called to love. We are not meant to hide from the world—if we did, how could we truly love family members and others who do not share our faith?

It might mean having an awkward conversation with a non-Catholic family member when they ask why Catholics use natural family planning (NFP), knowing how countercultural it is not to use contraception. It might mean sharing a Catholic article that I wrote on my personal Facebook page, knowing that friends will not approve. It might mean serving on a nonprofit board of directors made up of people of varying (or no) faith. Whatever way God calls me to share the Gospel, I know that I will only have the courage to do so if I ground myself in prayer.

We can enrich our faith life with relationships with other Catholics, raise our children to follow Jesus and his Church, *and* evangelize in whatever way he calls us to. Delphine Chui shows where faith may lead us when we heed that call.

Delphine Chui: Could a Conversion Cost Your Career?

Delphine Chui is a British writer. For over a decade, she wrote for major women's magazines, but she started feeling a little lost in a "circle of just striving."

She looked for fulfillment in nonprofit work by starting a charity, which she still runs today. It brought her joy and contentment—and taught her entrepreneurial skills—but didn't fulfill her.

"It was somewhere in that journey, muddled up, where I finally found God again, very strongly, and came back home to my Catholic faith," Delphine said. "And that's when things started to shift quite radically for me."

A growing misalignment between her faith and her work came to a head when Delphine attended a pro-life launch party and posted about it on her personal Instagram. "After that, it was like, to use Biblical language, it was like an exodus of just all the magazine editors who were commissioning me just unfollowed me, stopped talking to me, stopped commissioning me."

Afterward, Delphine said, she lost her voice: "For about six months, I just was quite stunted, and I didn't know what to do and how to move. I was a bit afraid to say anything . . . to the point where I didn't want to write anymore. I didn't want to create anymore, because I just [felt like I'd] been backed into a corner."

Fast-forward to today, and Delphine is happier than she's ever been. She examines every opportunity by asking, "Is this giving glory to God?" If the answer is no, then she says "no." This prayerful discernment has led her to a full-time job in communications for a Christian legal advocacy organization working for freedom of speech, freedom of religious belief, and right to life in Britain.

Delphine doesn't regret everything about her previous career. She learned a lot that she's now using in a way that's more aligned with her values and faith. As a result, she thinks that if a young woman has the opportunity to take a job in a major corporation in a way that does not make her lose herself and her faith, she should consider taking it.

Overall, the most important piece of advice Delphine has for women building a career in a secular field is to "be Catholic first . . . and then that will always help you make the right business decisions."

Spiritual Warfare

Si vis pacem, para bellum. If you want peace, prepare for war.

At first, this phrase, which I (Elise) came across in a talk by Fr. Mike Schmitz, struck me as dramatic and stark. However, as I've gone through various stages of my career, the "stakes" have gotten higher, and I've noticed an increased amount of spiritual warfare in my life. Whenever you answer "yes" to the Lord's calling to your life and remain steadfast in that calling, you will be met with opposition. Whether that "yes" seems small or large, by striving for God's will, you are participating in a greater story of salvation.

Here's what the Church has to say about spiritual warfare: "This dramatic situation of the whole world, which is in the power of the evil one, makes man's life a battle: The whole of man's history has been the story of dour combat with the powers of evil, stretching, so our Lord tells us, from the very dawn of history until the last day" (*CCC* 409).

We don't mention spiritual warfare to alarm or shock you, but as lay Catholic working women, it is an aspect of our faith that we need to be aware of in our daily lives. In chapter 2, we discussed discernment; it is within our father/daughter relationship with the Lord that we are attentive to his guidance in our daily lives. It is with that same attentiveness that we must be conscious of obstructions that can prevent us from living out his will for us.

Thankfully, we belong to a Church that has thousands of years of experience and wisdom to share with us when it comes to discernment and spiritual warfare. During his conversion, St. Ignatius of Loyola was inspired to develop a method of "discerning spirits": "He did not consider nor did he stop to examine this difference until one day his eyes were partially opened and he began to wonder at this difference and to reflect upon it. From experience he knew that some thoughts left him sad while others made him happy, and little by little he came to perceive the different spirits that were moving him; one coming from the devil, the other coming from God."[5]

St. Ignatius articulated the difference between "spiritual consolation" and "spiritual desolation." When we are experiencing spiritual consolation, we feel close to God and aligned with his graces. When we are experiencing spiritual desolation, we feel a spiritual dryness and darkness. The key in making sense of these movements is asking two questions: Where is this feeling coming from? Where is it leading me? In his Spiritual Exercises, Ignatius explains that good and evil spirits operate in accordance with the state of an individual's soul. There are fourteen rules of discernment, though you don't have to memorize each of these rules to find discernment of spirits useful in your everyday life. We recommend tools such as Fr. Timothy Gallagher's book *The Discernment of Spirits: An Ignatian Guide for Everyday Living* and the ones mentioned in chapter 2 to sharpen your discernment skills.

Living in Tension between Faith and Business

If you work in a secular workplace, you most likely have felt some tension between your faith and your workplace. Maybe someone was confused and seemed judgmental when you mentioned a lifestyle choice of yours that was influenced by your faith. Maybe you disagree with a coworker's choices for his or her family. Maybe you received strange looks when you told people about a retreat you went on or a Mass you attended. We've spoken with women who chose to leave a company because its leaders made a decision that was contradictory to the Catholic faith. There have been other women who disagree with some of the company's decisions or values but didn't have the financial means to leave. Amy Suzanne Upchurch, for her part, discovered how to bring Christian values to her distinctive women's health brand.

Amy Suzanne Upchurch: Leading a Christian Brand in a Secular Industry

Amy Suzanne Upchurch hadn't planned on becoming an entrepreneur, but after experiencing three challenging pregnancies due to hyperemesis gravidarum, she started looking for alternative approaches to treating the illness. "And I had a completely different pregnancy," she told Taryn on the *Catholic*

Women Lead podcast. "I didn't deal with morning sickness. I didn't go to the hospital."

"And so, I just felt called by God to start . . . a company that would come alongside and help women in their journey in pregnancy as they are dealing with different health issues," Amy said.

The company, Pink Stork, has since expanded into other areas of women's health. Today, their products are sold on their website as well as at Amazon, Walmart, and Target. Perhaps surprisingly, given that they are at those major retailers, Pink Stork's website and social media are explicitly Christian. Amy is public about her faith and has recently also started advocating for children, including the unborn, with Down syndrome, after her sixth child was diagnosed with the genetic disorder.

"I have had some negative reactions and comments," she said, "but . . . I try not to take it [personally], and I pray for them!"

Amy said that her faith has always informed her business decisions. "[My faith] touches everything," she said. "Jesus walks [the] extra mile for us," so she and her team do the same for their customers. For example, they include handwritten cards in all of their packages.

Amy does it for her employees, too. Because the mission of the company is to support and empower women, she said she makes sure she's supporting and empowering not only her customers but also her employees. She offers flexible work schedules, and her office is equipped with changing tables and spaces for babies and children to play.

"I don't want them to pick between being a mother and working," she said. She doesn't pick, either. Pink Stork started in a garage in her home on a military base, and her life as a wife and mother and her life as a business leader continue to be integrated. "It's authentic to who we are as a brand," she said. "It's been [a great blessing] that I've been able to empower women who are growing a career and [are] also moms."

Navigating the secular workplace as a Catholic can be exhausting at times. It's a constant discernment of how to till the garden that you've been given. Some women feel comfortable sharing about their faith without hesitation. Others need the safety of more developed relationships with coworkers in order to share their faith life. Either way is OK. The important point here is that you bring your whole self to work as a working Catholic woman. Trust in yourself and in God's calling for your life.

Over the course of writing this chapter and asking ourselves what to speak to regarding working in a secular workplace, one simple truth continued to return to us: Pray for them. Pray for your coworkers. Pray for your manager. Pray for your CEO. Pray for your customers or clients. You can be Christ's hands and feet in the world by placing them before God in prayer and asking for his blessing upon them. There is a deep beauty and power in believing and trusting that your prayers have real consequences for someone else's life. You may never see the fruit of those prayers this side of heaven, but you can trust in the benevolence of God, who listens and grants good things to those who ask of him, with "good measure, pressed down, shaken together, running over" (Lk

6:38). We are laborers in the vineyard of the world, and the Lord wants to help us harvest.

Questions for Reflection and Discussion

1. Are you experiencing any tension between your work and your values? Sit with this tension in prayer, perhaps in front of the Blessed Sacrament. How is the Lord calling you to respond?
2. How can you explicitly or implicitly share God's love with your coworkers?
3. When you hear the words "spiritual warfare," what comes to mind? What does that warfare look like in your particular situation?
4. Have you ever felt pressured to leave your faith at home, rather than bringing it into the office? How did you respond at the time? Would you do anything differently today?
5. Do you pray for the people you work with? How can you incorporate their intentions into your daily or weekly prayer routine?

SIX

HOW DO I JUGGLE FAITH, WORK, AND FAMILY?

> You can be a warrior, but you do not need to be a superhero.[1]
>
> Stephanie Kramer in *Carry Strong*

At Catholic Women in Business, we frequently have video calls with small children. Three of the four members of the leadership team, as of this writing, have a child or children under three. While we try to schedule meetings for after bedtime or during nap times, it doesn't always happen. And we're OK with that. We believe that a pro-woman company is a pro-family company, and "family" encompasses children, spouses, parents, grandparents, siblings . . . anyone for whom a team member cares.

There are challenges that come with being both part of a family and part of a business, but it's part and parcel of being a human being. Sometimes, it's meant postponing a project or rescheduling a meeting. Other times, it's meant having noise in the background or coloring with a toddler while leading a meeting. We could have grown much more quickly if we could dedicate all of our time to Catholic Women in Business, but we have family members to take care of. And they've always come second (after our faith).

How do you build a career that enables you to prioritize your faith and your family? How do you discern childcare decisions? How do you prioritize prayer and the sacraments in the midst of a busy life? How do you plan for maternity leave? How do you return to full-time work after taking time off to care for a child or children or for another family member? How do you work with children around? What does authentic, Christian self-care look like? If you are a business owner or work in human resources, how can you ensure that your organization supports working parents and other caregivers?

This chapter will answer these questions. Our hope is that throughout the next few pages, we can lay it all out there for you: the good, bad, and ugly of being called to both motherhood and business. This is messy. We are in no way the model for working women; we are simply trying to follow the Lord's direction for our lives and hope to love as much as possible along the way.

Managing Transitions

Taryn

"You're such a pro!" I was sitting on the floor in our nursery, giving my daughter a bottle and onboarding a new writer onto the Catholic Women in Business writing team. I'd planned ahead, preparing the bottle I knew she'd need so that it was right next to us while I was meeting this new writer. I'd recently started taking these calls, if my daughter wasn't napping, from the floor, where I could make sure she was playing safely while I chatted with the women who were joining our team.

I quickly dismissed the compliment, but it stuck with me. After almost seven months of trying to figure out how to juggle motherhood and work, it *was* feeling more natural.

When I left corporate America two weeks before my due date, I posted on LinkedIn and emailed clients and contacts, letting them know that I was leaving full-time work to be a stay-at-home mom and that I'd be freelancing as I was able. My plan was vague: Continue my work as an editor with Catholic Women in Business, and freelance . . . maybe? I had no idea what to expect.

After I'd gotten through the first six weeks, I settled into a rhythm. My daughter was a champion napper, and I had predictable blocks of two or three hours in which to work. I spent that time doing household chores, editing, writing, planning social media content, and resting. It was great. And it didn't last.

The next year was a series of unplanned schedule changes, unpredictable nap schedules, and uncertainty about how and when I'd be able to work. Many days, I'd cry to my husband, "I'll never be able to write again!" My usual dramatic flair had an edge of postpartum anxiety, but underneath the hyperbole was a real concern: *Who am I without my work? Can I have a fulfilling life without it? Would I have to?*

With experience (and a steadier nap schedule as my daughter got older and went down to one nap per day), I gained confidence in myself and trust in God's plan for my career. I learned to strive for balance in my desires—to hold onto my career goals loosely and listen to what God had in mind for my time and my work. I have days when it all feels too hard to juggle and I am tempted to give up any work that isn't homemaking and caregiving, and I have moments where I want to find paid work and childcare. In those moments, I stop and reflect: Is this what God's calling me to, or am I afraid that he isn't equipping me for my current season of life? So far, the answer has always been, "This is where I'm supposed to be—and he will provide."

I'm very fortunate that my husband earns enough money that we don't have to rely on my income, so we have the ability to make whichever childcare choice is best for our family. We moved out of the city to be able to afford housing on his salary and cut costs wherever we can. We don't know if Catholic school will be achievable. The point, though, isn't what we have, where we live, or whether or not we pay for childcare. The point is that we believe we've discerned God's will for us in the current season of our life, and we're doing what we can to follow it. As this book goes to press, we're preparing for the birth of our second child. What I'm not preparing for is any particular schedule. I know it will be unpredictable, I know it will change on a dime, and I know that I'll be able to accomplish whatever God wants me to accomplish—with his help.

"New School" Motherhood

Elise

I always knew that I wanted to work and have a family, but I didn't really think about the "working mom" part. I grew up with a stay-at-home mom, and words can't express how grateful I am for her devotion to my formation. I wouldn't be the woman I am today without her hard work of raising me and my siblings day in and day out. My dad was a lawyer and entrepreneur, so she often had long days of single parenting. Looking back, I have no idea how she kept up with the dinners, sports, dance practices, homework, and carpooling all of those years. She was always available for us whenever we needed her. She poured her whole heart into her children. She was and always will be my model for motherhood.

When I gave birth to my first daughter and was on the phone with my business partner a month after giving birth, asking for updates, I had no template. What did it mean to be a working mother? I felt like I was grasping for some sort of guidebook. I looked for women entrepreneurs in their fifties and sixties who were Catholic, had large families, and were happily married, and I woefully came up short.

For millennial and Gen Z women, even if our moms worked outside the home, our careers today look vastly different than those of our mothers. Maybe we saw our moms working on a desktop computer, but having constant availability to our work through our phones presents a completely new minefield to navigate. We are constantly tethered to people who need something from us. The more you grow in leadership, the more responsibilities you take on. The nonstop pace of having a career in 2024 requires us to have extremely strong judgment in how to set boundaries and navigate relationships.

This is going to look different for all of us. As Taryn mentioned, what's important is that you are equipped with the tools and courage you need to discern what is right for you, your marriage, and your family in every season in life.

The End of the Mommy Wars?

I (Taryn) never really know how to describe myself when it comes to my motherhood. Am I a stay-at-home mom? After all, I am our daughter's primary caregiver, and I rarely have childcare. Am I a working mom? After all, I (with Elise) lead a business and do my own freelancing as well. Am I some amalgam of the two? In a digital, post-COVID environment, where more and more mothers can work remotely and part time, do we need a new term?

Since the 1960s, a so-called "mommy war" has been raging, a fabricated battle between "stay-at-home moms" and "working moms." Perhaps in an attempt to justify our own decisions (which always come with drawbacks and challenges), we often feel the need to put down the decisions other women and mothers make. "Working moms," it's said, are giving their children to other people to raise, building a career to the detriment of their family. "Stay-at-home moms," it's said, are lazy or unambitious and don't care about the role model they're giving their daughters.

Of course, none of these statements is true. Childcare providers care for, but don't raise, the children they work with, and any mother can be a good role model for her daughter. Even the terms we use are inaccurate; every mother works, and no mother is trapped at home (though, arguably, in such isolated times as we live in, many "stay-at-home" moms feel lonely without the village that women mothered in for most of human history).

Fortunately, post-COVID, more mothers are opting out of the mommy wars, thanks to the rise of remote and flexible work, an increase in entrepreneurship among mothers, improved (although there's still lots of room for improvement) childcare and maternity leave options, and a new understanding of the challenges that all mothers face. In a culture that doesn't always provide effective support to mothers, more of us are providing that support to each other.

Entering Motherhood

My husband and I (Taryn) welcomed our first daughter in 2021. Throughout my pregnancy, my company was fully remote. I didn't have to commute with morning sickness, and I spent the whole pregnancy working from a recliner. (My coworkers didn't get to share the joy of my growing belly; they could only see me from the neck up!) While we were still discerning my work situation, my husband and I toured quite a few local daycares—all virtually. I worried both about how our daughter would stay safe at daycare during a pandemic and how she would fare emotionally and cognitively if her teachers all wore masks. I know many other mothers who shared these concerns and, as the pandemic continued, found themselves making difficult choices and midcourse adjustments to address the unique work- and family-related challenges of this time.

Pregnancy can be unpredictable, and the ways it will impact your work and career can be unpredictable, too. When to share the news of your pregnancy, whether to return to work after having a baby, whether to hire in-home childcare or use a daycare, whether to find a new job with better benefits, whether to decrease your hours, whether to take unpaid leave in addition to any paid maternity leave your employer offers (or instead of, in the event that you're at one of many companies that don't offer any) . . . there are a lot of decisions to discern, and no one answer is right for every family. The keys are prayer, planning, and support.

In her book *Carry Strong: An Empowered Approach to Navigating Pregnancy and Work*, L'Oréal executive and mother of two Stephanie Kramer shares a framework for navigating career and motherhood. It includes five principles: perspective, balance, community, communication, and identity. It also walks the reader through five phases through which each principle is woven: pre-preconception (before trying to conceive, or BTTC), trying to conceive (TTC), the hush (from the positive pregnancy test to the public announcement), the push (after sharing your news), and anticipating the great return (or not). Each phase requires consideration and planning—but you can feel empowered to know that motherhood can make you stronger and more confident, starting at conception: "I felt brave and bold *while* I was scared and hesitant—recognizing that strength was liberating and galvanizing. I started to recognize that my pregnancy at work had pushed me to learn perspective and balance with my own ambition in a way that was not constraining but propelling."[2]

Returning to Work

When my (Taryn's) younger sister started kindergarten, my mom, who'd been a "stay-at-home mom" for the previous decade, started teaching again—at the same school we went to, which made logistics a lot easier! From then until my sister graduated from high school, my mom was in and out of the workforce, depending on the needs of the family. Now, she sometimes jokes that she's retired from her career as a stay-at-home mom and teaches "for fun."

Maybe you took years off to care for your children full time until they left for college. Maybe you took off a few years during their early childhood. Maybe you needed to take a step back from your career to care for elderly parents or a disabled family member. Or, maybe you've just left the workforce for full-time caregiving and are wondering what you can do in the meantime so you're prepared to return when the time comes.

The bad news is that the rate of workplace change is faster than ever. The good news is that there is also more support than ever for women returning to the workforce. The momentum was building before 2020, but 2020–2021 saw a "she-cession"[3] stemming from school closures and business closures in female-dominated industries.[4] As a result, the last few years have seen a huge influx of women returning to work after taking a break for months or even years.

Programs such as "returnships"—internships for people (often mothers) returning to the workforce—can be a great help in finding and training for a new job.[5] Such programs are growing in popularity at major employers, and there are multiple organizations that assist companies in setting them up.

There's also a growing recognition of the skills women hone when they are stay-at-home moms—skills that are transferable to a variety of jobs. LinkedIn made waves in 2022 when it added "stay-at-home mom," "stay-at-home dad," and "stay-at-home parent" to its list of possible job titles for users to put on their profiles. On your resume and in interviews, be sure to share about volunteer roles you've taken on (PTA board service is no joke!) and leadership skills you've developed as a mother. I know I'm better at prioritizing tasks, communicating, and task-switching since I had my daughter.

A Day in the (Real) Life of a Working Mother

Elise

My hope for this chapter is to really dive deep into the messiness of working mom life. Maybe you already have a cohort of friends who are working moms, but if not, I want to offer you some encouragement and hope. We see incredible videos and photos online of polished women who are organized for the day and jet off to exciting and fulfilling jobs while their kids are perfectly content with their form of childcare.

I can tell you that is not what our current season of life looks like! My husband and I both work for our family's law firm. As a young defense attorney, my husband is currently working sixty to seventy hours per week. My schedule is more flexible as a C-suite member, but I am usually working forty hours minimum, inside and outside the home, between two businesses. I am thankful that we live in an area that is close to my mom and our work and only three hours from extended family, who visit often. We have a full-time nanny who has become like family to us. Both girls are currently at home, although they do have weekly activities like swim lessons and gymnastics.

Here's what a typical day in the life looks like for me as an executive, wife, and mom:

- *5:30 a.m.:* I pull myself out of bed to squeeze in at least twenty minutes of quiet and prayer with coffee before the day gets started.
- *6 a.m.–7 a.m.:* My oldest, Rosemary, wakes up usually exactly at six, if not a few minutes before. When Emilia wakes up, we settle into books, breakfast, prayer, and television while I get ready for the day.

- *7:30 a.m.:* At least a couple of days a week, Hunter takes the girls so I can go to the gym or take a walk in our neighborhood. In order for me to physically take care of my children, I also need to pursue my own health as well. Our nanny arrives around 8 a.m.
- *10 a.m.–12 p.m.:* In the mornings, I usually meet with my six direct reports. A couple of times a month, I attend one of the girls' morning activities: library story time, swim lesson, or gymnastics lesson.
- *2 p.m.–5 p.m.:* This is when I do concentrated strategic work or have more meetings. Once a quarter, I work with our department heads to create goals for each department. I check on the progress of those goals weekly. We also have Individual Development Plans for each executive, so I review them to see what needs to be moved forward that week or day to help our company leaders grow.
- *5 p.m.–6 p.m.:* I get home between five and six. Usually, on Sundays, I try to meal-prep dishes that our nanny can pop in the oven to heat up so that they're ready when I get home. However, we do rely on takeout and frozen food at least a couple times a week.
- *6 p.m.–8 p.m.:* This is concentrated family time. I put my phone away (although this doesn't always happen, and I am sometimes tying up a loose end from an ongoing conversation!). We do dinner together as a family (which is absolutely chaotic with two toddlers!), bath time, prayers, books, and bed.
- *8 p.m.–10 p.m.:* This is my time to regroup for the next day. I straighten up the house with Hunter. Most nights, he goes back to work, but a couple times a week, we're able to spend some time together before bed. Sometimes, I use this time for writing or a Catholic Women in Business meeting.

There are so many caveats to this schedule. We are in a particular season of family life where I am able to have devoted time to exercise and pray alone. I know that when and if I'm pregnant again, that mostly won't be the case (I had hyperemesis gravidarum with both of my past pregnancies). We live in constant change. We'll go a stretch of a month or two with no illnesses, and then all of a sudden, all four of us have the flu, and we're back in survival mode.

How do I keep things moving forward when life gets like this? For many of us, like our friend Shivonne Sant-Solomon, the key is remembering your values.

Shivonne Sant-Solomon: From Working Mom to Stay-at-Home Mom . . . and Back Again

Shivonne Sant-Solomon is a business leader from Trinidad and Tobago who has worked in the energy industry for her entire career, spanning twenty years.

When she and her husband had their first child, she told us, "Career priorities shifted. Immediately." Shivonne and her husband were both working in the demanding energy industry at a company and had a significant commute, but they had help with childcare.

Then, they received the opportunity for an overseas assignment in Australia, where they had no support system. Shivonne became her son's full-time caregiver and earned her MBA during the two years they were there. She returned to work in Trinidad and Tobago and then had another child, ultimately deciding to take another step back.

Despite her belief that it was the right decision, Shivonne still felt lost that first day she didn't go to work. "I felt as if my identity was taken away from me," she said. The transition took some time, but then, she said, she found joy. She was a full-time caregiver for a little over three years and recommends it for anyone who has the opportunity. She returned to work in order to earn income for her children's education fund and found a job that didn't require a commute.

However, she felt taken advantage of because she felt the need to prove herself after having been out of the workforce. That stress, combined with the pandemic, led her to quit that job—without having another job lined up. "I went full obedience and trust in God," she said.

During Shivonne's time off, she started working toward a coaching certification through a Christian coaching organization. Now, she's back in the energy industry in a job where she only has to commute a few days a week. On the other mornings, she is able to set aside time for prayer and exercise and her children.

Shivonne has had male colleagues tell her that she is inspiring to their wives as they take a break from paid work to care for children but hope to reenter the workforce one day.

"You know, sometimes there's these feelings of imposter syndrome," she said. "'Can I really do this? Do they expect that from me?' [But] God's grace has placed you here. And he knows the sacrifices that you have made."

Understand Your MVPs

Shivonne Sant-Solomon told us that she likes to recommend that women do what she calls an MVP, based on an exercise she did in her coach training program. It stands for mission, values, and purpose, and

Shivonne said her teachers taught her to put a time stamp on her MVP because it will change.

Understanding your mission, your values, and your purpose can help you prioritize. Keep in mind that our ultimate mission is to join Christ in heaven after we die—but what are some shorter-term missions? What is your mission in your career? What values do you bring to your work? What do you believe is your purpose in working—what is it that God is calling you to do through your work?

The answers to these questions, as Shivonne said, will vary throughout the course of your career. But knowing what they are at any given time will help you identify which tasks and activities to prioritize.

A Working Mom's Rule of Life

Elise

Being open and not hardened to constant change has been one of the most difficult parts of motherhood for me. However, I have found that having a loose "rule of life" as a working mom has been incredibly helpful. A rule of life is a schedule, routine, or rhythm of the day aimed at helping us to live out our vocation. As a type A person, I *love* to plan. I have loved the idea of a rule of life since I was single, when it looked something like having almost every hour of my day planned. However, I've had to adapt this thinking as I've grown in my vocations to work and motherhood.

What has helped is to know the two or three things that must get done within my day to know that I'm fulfilling my call as wife and mother and filling my cup so that I can serve others. Usually, that list consists of praying a daily Rosary; working out; spending intentional, quiet time with my girls; making a phone call to a friend; attending Mass; saying Night Prayer with Hunter; and spending an intentional ten to fifteen minutes with my husband. If I can prioritize two or three things from that list per day, I know I am aligned with my vocations.

I would love to get to the point again where I can have a more structured rule of life, but I know that it's not possible with this current season of work and family—and that's OK. The temptation to be too rigid with my schedule and become frustrated by the natural changes that have to occur day to day because of family life is something I'm continually working on. However you currently approach work, faith, and family, know that the Lord is always there to help you reevaluate your schedule and lend inspiration to discerning your next steps.

Stephanie Kramer writes in *Carry Strong* that you can do it all—but not all at the same time. You also can't do it without help! In our experience, there are three Ps that will help you juggle your prayer life, your family responsibilities, and your work: *prayer*, *prioritization*, and *partners*.

Prayer

Taryn

I realized soon after I became pregnant that there was no way I would be the mother my daughter needed on my own, or even with support from my husband (who is the best husband and father I've ever known!). The only way to do it, I'm convinced, is with prayer. I *can* be a good mother—but only in him who strengthens me (Phil 4:13).

The most important thing you can do as a working mother (or working caregiver of any kind) is pray. Of course, as a working mother, it's also hard to find time to pray! The best tool I've found to help me prioritize prayer is, strange as it may sound, the notes and reminders apps on my iPhone. I have recurring reminders each morning to say a short prayer to renew my Marian consecration, to say the guardian angel prayer for my daughter and me, and to pray for everyone on my prayer intentions list (which is in a note). I also used the reminders app to start praying a daily Rosary; eventually, I reached a point where the habit is so ingrained that I don't need the reminder anymore. (You can also start with just a decade if you're new to this devotion but want to build up to a daily Rosary.)

My husband and I also set aside time in the evening for journaling. In fact, I use his journaling to remind me to do it myself! My journaling routine consists of a "3 x 5 Examen," which I learned from Fr. Mark-Mary of the Franciscan Friars of the Renewal.[6] I write down five things I'm grateful for, five things I ask for forgiveness for, and five petitions. (Depending on the day, it might be more than five or fewer than five, but the goal is five.) Simply writing down what I am grateful for at the end of the day helped me with postpartum mood challenges. Adding in the examination of conscience is a great way for me to continually work on growing in virtue and helps me do a better examination of conscience before I go to Confession. (I returned to the sacrament when I was twenty-eight. It was hard but worth it, and I've encountered the Holy Spirit many times through the priest in the Confessional.)

I frequently have to remind myself that my relationship with Jesus is my top priority, because, all too often, it doesn't feel like it. I have a million other things to do, it seems, and sitting down for prayer feels like a luxury I don't have. And it's true that as a busy mom, I try to pray on the go (Rosaries while folding laundry, for instance!) and turn my least favorite tasks into offerings. But nothing replaces that quiet prayer time, and as I've heard many other Catholics point out, when I make time for prayer, Jesus makes sure I have time for everything else he's asking me to do.

Elise

A theme in my prayer life that I have come back to time and time again over the past few years is the idea of finding silence amid chaos. Spiritual warriors such as Jacques Philippe, St. Elizabeth of the Trinity, St. John of the Cross, and Catherine Doherty have led me to a practical model of how to "pray constantly" (1 Thes 5:17).

Now, I have to tell you, I am lucky if I get twenty minutes of silent prayer each day. Hunter and I usually attend daily Mass once a week and, of course, Mass on Sunday. We attend Confession once a month and try to make time for adoration a handful of times per year. We have really struggled to adjust our prayer time together post-kids. Before children, we prayed a weekly Rosary together and prayed an Angelus and Night Prayer every night. Now, with toddlers, although we strive to be consistent, those prayers are more sporadic.

What has really helped me feel as if I'm still progressing in my prayer life is finding my inner "poustinia," as Catherine Doherty described it (see chapter 7). Operating out of charity and grace in our daily tasks requires us to be steeped in an inner silence where we can hear the Lord's voice and deeply know his presence.

"All of this standing still can be done in the midst of the outward noise of daily living and the duties of state in life. For it will bring order into the soul, God's order, and God's order will bring tranquility, his own tranquility. And it will bring silence . . . the silence will come and take possession of love, bride, mother, nurse, apostle, priest, nun—if only the face of their soul, in the midst of their daily occupations, is turned to God."[7]

I find micromoments throughout my day to talk to my Creator, to tell him my frustrations, joys, and whatever else is on my heart. It might just be a quick moment of attuning to his voice, but it's in that brief time that I tune out all the other noise in my head and find peace. This moment fuels me to keep going and focus on the task at hand.

Prioritization

The second P is where the concept of time stewardship (from chapter 1) comes into play. To steward your time well, you have to prioritize. What is God calling you to do in each moment? It's easy to think he doesn't care about every second of your day—after all, doesn't he have better things to do?—but the truth is, he is outside of time and therefore doesn't have to prioritize in the same way we do. In other words, he does care about every moment of your life.

There have been times while writing this book when we wanted to be working on the book but had more urgent things to do—other work tasks, childcare, cooking, or even leisure activities. There have been other times when we felt like there was something else we should be doing but knew that in that moment, we should be writing.

Prioritizing sometimes means taking time for self-care. As a Christian, a businesswoman, and possibly a wife, mother, or both, there are a lot of demands on your time and energy. Remember that God gave you your body and your mind to cherish and use wisely. As St. Paul wrote, "Do you not know that your body is a temple of the Holy Spirit within you, which you have from God? You are not your own; you were bought with a price. So glorify God in your body" (1 Cor 6:19–20).

In an interview on the *Market Your Genius* podcast, Julie Cole, founder of Mabel's Labels and mother of six, said that she has a checklist she uses before saying "yes" to an opportunity, such as speaking at an event. Before she agrees to give someone her time, she makes sure the opportunity checks all of those boxes.[8] Your boxes might include things like being able to pick your children up from school or tuck them into bed, keeping a weekly Holy Hour commitment, or ensuring that the organization or person offering you the opportunity has values aligned with yours. Whatever they are, using this checklist can help make sure you're keeping your priorities in order—as St. Zélie Martin did in her own pursuit of holiness.

St. Zélie Martin: Balancing Life by Keeping God in the Center

Marie-Azélie "Zélie" Guérin was born in 1831 in France. She wanted to join the religious life but was turned away due to her poor health. In 1851, she heard a voice tell her, "Undertake the making of Point d'Alençon lace." She dedicated herself to this work and to praying for her vocation—now understood to be marriage.

In 1858, when she was twenty-six, she saw a man crossing a bridge and heard a voice say, "This is he whom I have prepared for you." The man was Louis Martin, a watchmaker, who had also initially felt called to religious life. They married a few months later and spent the first ten months of their marriage living in a celibate (Josephite) marriage.

A spiritual director encouraged them to have children, however, and they did—nine in thirteen years. They lost four as young children, which caused a great deal of grief. All five of their surviving daughters became nuns: Marie, Pauline, Céline, and their youngest, Thérèse, became Carmelites in the same convent. Their middle daughter, Léonie, had some behavioral difficulties, appears to have been developmentally delayed, was abused by their maid, and ultimately attempted to enter religious life multiple times before finally entering the Visitation Order.

Thérèse was canonized in 1925 and named a Doctor of the Church in 1997. Louis and Zélie were canonized in 2015, the first married couple with children to be canonized together. And, the cause for Léonie's canonization was opened in 2015, giving her the title "Servant of God."

Zélie, despite being comfortably well-off, had a difficult life. She ran a successful and therefore demanding business; in fact, Louis ended up closing his business to join hers. The family was also busy with Church and philanthropic work: Zélie was a Third Order Franciscan and member of several other Catholic groups, and the Martins observed all of the Church's fasting requirements and guidelines, went to Mass at 5:30 each morning, received the Eucharist as often as they could, and filled their days with prayer.

Zélie died of breast cancer at age forty-five, becoming a wonderful model and intercessor for any woman who is trying to balance work and family life while keeping God at the center of everything she does.

Partners

Taryn

As we discussed in chapter 4, we were not made to live life alone. Even if you're not married, you likely have family members—whether related by blood or chosen in friendship. You have coworkers—or, if you're a solopreneur, you have other people you encounter through your work. The best way to manage a busy life is with the support of other people.

For me, becoming a stay-at-home mom during a pandemic was an isolating experience. Between trying to keep my family healthy and adjusting to not seeing adults (other than my husband) every day, I was lonely for about the first year. But then, we bought a house and settled into a new community. My daughter's routine had become more predictable, and there was more time for us to get out together. I started what I call a Bible Study Playgroup by posting in a local Facebook group and texting a couple of moms I knew. Every Thursday morning, we meet at my house for Bible study—kids included.

As I write this, we have a group of six moms and a growing group of children ages newborn to three. It's the most chaotic Bible study you'll ever see. It's full of interruptions, but I have my mom village. Some of us work part time, and some have stopped working altogether to focus on family life. Some have one child, and others have more than one. We've shared chronic illnesses, births, miscarriages, fertility concerns, potty-training mishaps, last-minute babysitting calls, and breastfeeding challenges. As I prepared for my second endometriosis surgery and hoped for another child, I knew that things would be so different this time around: I had people I could call for help.

The internet has made us more isolated than ever before; too often, we settle for weak online ties rather than rich, real relationships. On the other hand, the internet also makes it easier than ever to build a village. Look for your local young adult's group, mom group, or Catholic women's group. If there isn't one—this part is crucial—start your own. I promise you there are other women who could use the friendship.

Elise

To be honest, I have struggled immensely to make new mom friends as a working mom. Most playgroups meet during working hours, and when I can occasionally attend an activity with the girls, I'm too focused on them to really open myself up to conversation with someone new. When we moved to the Baltimore area in spring 2021, I tried to start a group of families to meet once a week for prayer and discussion. Despite my efforts, the Lord made it clear that it wasn't the season for a group like this to form. We decided we'll revisit this idea as we continue to settle into our community.

Right now, we have a smaller group of really wonderful friends. We have a group of immediate friends in the area and a larger group of friends sprinkled throughout the country; we speak to them a handful of times a year and visit every so often. However, we know that we are all connected by prayer and the Eucharist. Investing in friendships of shared faith has been a great comfort as we have shouldered joys and struggles together over the years.

My marriage and partnership with Hunter has also looked different throughout the ever-changing seasons of work, faith, and family life. Hunter has always been the biggest supporter and encourager in my career. After many years of grad school, law school, clerkships, and entrepreneurship, we're now entering into business together with different roles at our family company. Working with your spouse could be the topic of a whole other book, but the challenge of navigating a new level of work-life balance has required an incredible amount of discernment and patience from us both. We have learned when to talk about work at home (we try to not bring it up around the girls), when to talk about family (we reserve the office for work discussions—not family, unless it's an emergency), and when we can talk about both (we have weekly lunch dates at a restaurant nearby so we can have a "neutral area" to talk about whatever is on our minds in work or family).

As I've gone back into an office job, I have also had to humbly learn how to communicate more when it comes to household duties. As I mentioned, I love homemaking and liturgical living, so I tend to overextend myself when it comes to tending to the house. Hunter is usually extremely gracious in equally sharing the household chores, but when it comes to things (such as laundry or the dishes) being done "my way," I've had to let go of perfectionism and accept "done" over "perfect."

I would be remiss in not also mentioning my business partner of the last five years, Claire Conway. Healthy, fruitful business partnerships are truly rare and require a tremendous amount of vulnerability and trust from both parties. It has been an honor to have a business partner who I know is invested not only in our business but also my personal and family life. Integrating faith, work, and family will always be a never-ending undertaking. Don't let that prevent you from striving to follow God's call in each area of your life.

How Can I Succeed at Work while Being Open to Life?

Elise

This is a question many women struggle with, so I didn't want to end the chapter without addressing it.

When I found out I was pregnant with my second, Emilia, my daughter Rosemary was barely six months old. I remember the morning so clearly: I was up early, Hunter had left for work, and I was working from home with Rosemary. I realized that it had been an unusually long time since my last period. I bundled up Rosemary, put her in the stroller, and walked the half mile to our local pharmacy, trying to clear my head. When we got home, I placed Rosemary on the bathroom floor and took the test; sure enough, it was positive.

I remember my world falling out from under me. My anxiety came on full force, and I had to put my head between my knees to catch my breath. This was not how I had imagined growing our family. I had just gotten back into the swing of things with work after my maternity leave. Hunter had just started a new job, and we were not financially stable enough to feel comfortable bringing a new baby into our family. I wrestled with feelings of anger, resentment, fear, excitement, guilt, stress, and worry for months. *How was I going to do this?*

I slowly realized that this was the wrong question to be asking. The Lord remained so close to our family over the next ten months as we prepared to welcome Emilia. He made it abundantly clear that I wasn't going to accomplish anything on my own. Once again, I came face-to-face with my own dependence on God and others. My heart was stretched beyond my comprehension as my belly grew. Slowly, my negative emotions turned to pure joy.

For married women, fertility is an important factor in career planning. As wives and mothers using NFP, Taryn and I keep our family planning in mind when planning for Catholic Women in Business—and always try to remember that God can change those plans; he knows what's best for us.

Our fertility highlights the core of the feminine genius: our receptivity and openness to others. As with every detail of our feminine genius, we are to bring all of ourselves to work, including our fertility. We cannot compartmentalize our fertility—and it takes an enormous amount of courage and trust. Through our feminine genius, we are reminded once again of Pope Benedict XVI's words: "Those who desire comforts have dialed the wrong number. Rather, [God] shows us the way to great things, the good, towards an authentic human life."[9]

Staying open to God's plan for your family and your work is a continuous process of discernment. The beauty of NFP means that you make a monthly decision about whether or not you need to try to avoid pregnancy (TTA). Sometimes, you may be in a long season of TTA. Other times, you may be in a long season of TTC (trying to conceive). Still other times, you may face an unexpected pregnancy or even be in a season of "TTW" ("trying to whatever").

We know a wide range of women using NFP. For some, the practice is easily incorporated into their marriage, work life, and personal life. For others, NFP is a tremendous cross and greatly impacts their everyday life. Wherever you are on this spectrum, know that you are not alone, and there is a community of women here to support you on your journey of integrating your work, faith, and family planning. Leah Darrow provides an inspiring example of how she finds that "balance."

Leah Darrow: The Dance of Work-Life Balance

Leah Darrow was a contestant on season 3 of *America's Next Top Model*, but she walked away from her modeling career after a dramatic return to the Catholic faith in the middle of a photo shoot, as depicted in her book.[10]

Since then, Leah has earned a master's degree in theology, had a successful career in public speaking, and had six children (plus two in heaven) with her husband. At her public speaking engagements, she found that what she loved most was answering questions afterward. She realized that God was calling her to have a one-on-one impact and therefore became a coach for Catholic mom entrepreneurs, which has also enabled her to stay home and spend more time with her family.

We asked Leah how she integrates her faith into her work, and she said, "There is no integration. . . . If you're a woman of faith, then you're a woman of faith in your business."

She continued, "It's how I speak to myself. It's how I speak to my husband, to my kids. It's how I interact with my clients. It's the integrity I have in my business and my products and the prices and all of it. So my faith is a part of everything."

We don't need to separate our dreams for our career from our dreams for our family, she said. "They go together. So, my dream to be a mom, my dream to be a wife, my dream for all of that, it's a part of these other dreams that God's also given me to do and talents he's given me to [use]."

Of course, she adds, you have to prioritize. Her dreams outside her family support her family, but they also come second to her roles as a wife and mother. What's more, Leah said, "Some seasons, I was able to really go full throttle on a career; sometimes, I'm pulling back, and that takes a tremendous amount of discernment and closeness to the Holy Spirit."

When we asked Leah what a work-life balance looks like for her, she rendered a metaphor: "Life and business are like a dance floor, and we're the dancers. We move to the rhythm of our responsibilities, our obligations, our dreams, our to-do list. And sometimes, it's a waltz, and it's smooth, and you know the steps, and it's effortless. You're like, 'This is amazing! It's happening!' . . . Other times, it feels like a fiery tango, where you're being whipped from one corner of the dance floor to the next, and you don't quite know what's going on." During a waltz season, the more formal, structured times, it's important to put in place a good prayer routine that helps you settle more deeply into prayer and keep you grounded during the tangos, which are more fluid and, potentially, free.

Questions for Reflection and Discussion

1. In terms of the three Ps, where do you feel like you have the best handle on things, and where could you be more intentional in setting yourself up for success?
2. Do you need to rethink how you've set up childcare, care for other family members, or your work hours? Whom can you talk to for guidance and support?
3. What skills have you learned from caregiving (for children or other loved ones)? How do they apply to the work you do (or want to do)?
4. How can you be more supportive of coworkers whose pregnancy is unexpected—and possibly unwelcome—news?
5. What is one way you can help build up a company culture that is truly family friendly?

SEVEN

HOW CAN I MAKE A DIFFERENCE AS A CATHOLIC ENTREPRENEUR?

> It's OK to feel our feelings and process and release them. We're told that "we don't bring emotion into the boardroom," but I think that is what makes female entrepreneurship so special and so impactful.[1]
>
> Mimi Striplin, founder of The Tiny Tassel and Parfaire Consulting

Elise

Even if you are not a business owner, don't skip ahead! We promise this chapter is still pertinent to you. Every profession involves some skills of an entrepreneur, including creativity.

Throughout many years of discernment about my career and its many twists and turns, one thing has become clear to me: I am an entrepreneur to my core. I have studied and created art since high school, and I was always curious how this creative part of myself would play into my career; I knew I didn't exactly want to be a painter or graphic designer, but I knew that my ability to generate something out of nothing was valuable. It wasn't until I read this quote from St. John Paul II that I started to understand how creativity and business worked together: "God therefore called man into existence, committing to him the craftsman's task. Through his 'artistic creativity' man appears more than ever 'in the image of God,' and he accomplishes this task above all in shaping the wondrous 'material' of his own humanity and then exercising creative dominion over the universe which surrounds him" (*Letter to Artists*, 1).

"Exercising creative dominion over the universe" is, succinctly, work. This means that through our work as Catholic businesswomen, we become "craftsmen," cocreating with God. St. John Paul II again describes the importance of this cocreation with God: "Not all are called to be artists in the specific sense of the term. Yet, as Genesis has it, all men and women are entrusted with the task of crafting their own life: in a certain sense, they are to make of it a work of art, a masterpiece" (*Letter to Artists*, 2).

Therefore, whether you own an LLC or are mostly a stay-at-home mom, as a human created in the image and likeness of God, you are called to work, whatever form that work takes. This work is active participation in the cocreative nature of your heavenly Father. Work is not a punishment. It was given to us before the fall of humanity (Gn 1:27–28) and is a purposeful gift from our Creator.

In this chapter, we will be exploring what it means to be a principled entrepreneur and how, as women, we have a particular approach to entrepreneurship through our spiritual motherhood. Before we begin, let's take a look at one example of someone who instills "principled entrepreneurship" in her family business and its beautiful results.

Laura Pugliano: Leading a Family Business with Authenticity and Faith

Laura Pugliano's story sounds like a Hallmark movie. As a third-generation Italian American, she'd always loved everything Italian. She studied in Italy in college, lived there for a while after college, and later, back in the United States, met and married an Italian. Now, they run a business—Ciccio's Olives—importing olive oil from her husband's family's farm in Calabria, Italy.

They have three children, and Laura also does some marketing consulting. She works in between caring for her children, supplementing with some childcare.

Laura's Catholic faith infuses every part of her work as an entrepreneur. She's not just selling olive oil to make money, she said. "We're doing it because we know that we can help them revive and rejuvenate communities in Southern Italy." Laura is also motivated by the delicious taste and the health benefits of pure olive oil, as opposed to the adulterated olive oils so prevalent in today's market. She wants to bring it to more consumers.

"We only look to authentic items of worth and value to bring to our store," Laura said. "The origin story of a product is just as important as the product itself. We must uphold the dignity of the worker and seek to positively impact others around the globe in any way we can."

Laura also spoke to the value of beauty. In addition to olive oil, Ciccio's Olives sells artisan products such as home goods and bath and body products. Having "beautiful things around us," she said, "can lift us up to Christ in a way." It's important to her that her company provides customers with this kind of beauty right in their own kitchens.

Finally, Laura spoke to the importance of authenticity—of knowing who you are and standing firm in that identity. But that self-awareness doesn't come internally, she pointed out: it comes from God.

Mary, for example, "knew who she was," Laura said, "but she also looked to God to tell her who she was. And then she was secure in that." And we need entrepreneurs who are, according to Laura, "ready to lead—women who are ready to stand strong in their faith and not be apologetic for it, women who can be elegant and can be faithful and can be professional all at the same time."

Principled Entrepreneurship

The concept of "principled entrepreneurship" was created by entrepreneur, business coach, and professor Andreas Widmer.[2] After beginning his career in the Swiss Army as a Swiss Guard to Pope John Paul II, Andreas went on to an illustrious international career in business. When he experienced a major business failure and burnout, he decided to embark on a new kind of business ownership, one that would put the customer and values before profit. In his book *The Art of Principled Entrepreneurship*, Andreas outlines five important principles that help to build a healthy, "people first" environment. Let's take a brief look at each of them here.

- *The Economy Exists for People, Not People for the Economy:* This pillar focuses on the question "How may I help you?" A principled entrepreneur "always concerns themselves with the customer's needs and provides a profitable solution."[3] Such companies value excellence, resilience, and curiosity.
- *To Work Is to Create; to Create Is to Be Human:* A principled entrepreneur "fosters an environment in which each person can flourish and excel—individually and as a group—through creation, lending

support, and offering fair and lasting rewards."[4] This fosters positive relationships that are essential to a healthy work environment.

- *Culture Eats Strategy for Breakfast:* Andreas defines culture as "what you do when no one is looking"[5] and quotes businessman Art Ciocca as saying, "Either create a strong culture or you'll have to manage tough."[6] Companies that instinctively put the needs of customers and employees first, building a culture of mutual trust, create a healthy environment without which employees cannot pursue excellence.
- *Principled Entrepreneurs Always Seek to Create Win-Win Solutions:* This sentiment echoes the saying often shared in entrepreneurial circles: "A rising tide lifts all boats." The underlying assumption of greed and scarcity is antithetical to the principled entrepreneur. "Business must always take a win-win approach—to other companies in your industry and to your employees."[7] This "narrow way" to business absolutely requires innovation, resourcefulness, and an abundance mindset.
- *Always Think Like an Entrepreneur:* Principled entrepreneurs are creators. They "focus on generating value, looking forward, and thinking of the next way the team or company can grow in excellence and create more value for customers."[8]

When a business is centered on the pursuit of human excellence and development, it does not have to apologize for generating profit. It is rightly ordered in first seeking to serve its founder, employees, and community. Likewise, when a business is conceived in a desire to serve and promote excellence, it can continue to thrive in others-centered work. Leah Jacobson heard such a call to serve as part of her mission of spiritual motherhood, a mission that is improving the lives of many women.

Leah Jacobson: Faithful Spiritual Motherhood in Entrepreneurship

Leah Jacobson never had a career plan or ambitions for a specific title or path. She didn't even have her current CEO title at the nonprofit she founded (Guiding Star Project, which provides life-affirming health care and education services) until they needed to list a CEO for a grant application. Now, she's also launching a graduate program in Catholic gender studies at the University of St. Thomas in Houston, Texas.

"It's just been purely, quite frankly, just 'Jesus, whatever you want me to do with my life,'" she told us. "I think, as I've moved through my career, I've had a higher risk tolerance, probably, than most, because I saw the Lord's faithfulness."

After working for several years in university ministry and then as a lactation consultant, Leah first heard God's call to start Guiding Star Project while she was in adoration. She didn't know how it was going to happen, she said, "but the Lord always answered my 'How?' with a 'who.' And he would bring the next person into my life [who] would take it to that next step."

Now, seventeen years later, Guiding Star Project serves women in seven locations in five states—and is growing. "It's starting to make sense now," Leah told us—but "it was close to fifteen years before I began to even pay myself . . . success doesn't necessarily translate into financial gain, you know?" Changing lives and building relationships make the hard work worth it to Leah.

"Sometimes," she said, "as a Catholic woman, especially if you're very faithful and you have obedience, you sometimes tend to shrink yourself just a tiny bit—because who am I? I'm not a priest, I'm not a bishop." But, as her female spiritual director told her, "The Church needs you to stand up and be vocal. The Church needs your voice."

"Our nature is to mother," Leah said. "We have this innate call upon our life to be a mother, physically, spiritually, in all the ways, to each other. And in entrepreneurship, especially, there can be so much self-doubt. There can be so much fear, so having another woman come alongside you and just say, 'You got it, it's OK,' that's very valuable. . . . [Spiritual motherhood] really is that accompaniment, that friendship . . . it's really just a ministry of presence."

Entrepreneurship and Spiritual Motherhood

Our work as women entrepreneurs is both intrinsically other-centered and inherently incarnational. We cannot build a business without being deeply changed: spiritually, emotionally, mentally, and physically. What we generate from our entrepreneurial projects has not only temporal effects but also eternal ones. Andreas writes, "The value we generate is both *within others*—in the products, services, and relationships we create—and *within ourselves*."[9] And through the lens of principled entrepreneurship, we experience business as an extension of our spiritual motherhood.

Elise

As someone who has started and led several companies, I can attest that entrepreneurship is an all-consuming endeavor. The ideas for my businesses came from my heart, and when push came to shove, the success and direction of Ringlet came down to my decisions. Entrepreneurship is stressful, with sleepless nights and worry, but I have been changed by the relationships that have been created through my work. The emotional and mental work that I pour into others through my work in business produces new life in others and myself. By stepping into this generative power gifted to me by God through entrepreneurship, I am answering the call of Jesus to go and bear fruit: "You did not choose me, but I chose you and appointed you that you should go and bear fruit and that your fruit should abide" (Jn 15:16).

Just as the Blessed Mother received the Holy Spirit in her womb and bore the Son of God, we, too, receive our vocation to business and bear into the world the fruit of this union between ourselves and God. The world needs this fruit! It desperately needs the goodness of your loving work, relationships, and faithfulness. We join our words to Mary in saying "Behold, I am the handmaiden of the Lord, let it be to me according to your word" (Lk 1:38).

Following is a beautiful example of how one woman's faithful response to God's call upon her life produced beautiful fruit for the kingdom of God.

Catherine de Hueck Doherty: A Friend to the Poor

Born into a wealthy Russian family in 1896, Ekaterina Fyodorovna Kolyschkina was baptized into the Russian Orthodox Church. When she was just fifteen, Catherine married her cousin Baron Boris de Hueck and became a baroness. (Their marriage was later annulled on the basis of the couple's familial relationship.)

After Catherine served as a nurse in World War I, she and her husband escaped the Russian Revolution by moving to Finland. They were later evacuated to England, where Catherine entered the Roman Catholic Church, and then immigrated to Canada, where she gave birth to their son, George.

In 1924, Catherine moved to New York and worked and lived in poverty as a laundress. However, after a friend invited the baroness to her Manhattan apartment to give a talk on Russia, she began a successful career as a lecturer, speaking across North America on Russia and communism.

When Catherine realized that Communists were able to persuade people to join their movement because of the very real needs of the poor, she started offering practical and spiritual help to the people the Communists targeted, "lifting up these beleaguered souls to God and interceding for their blessing" (John Paul II, ***Letter to Women***). In 1934, Catherine founded Friendship House in Toronto, expanding it to Harlem in 1938 and Chicago in 1942. Her marriage annulled, she married American journalist and twice-widowed Eddie Doherty in 1943, and together they took up the work of advocacy and service among the poor.

A disagreement with the other leaders of Friendship House in Chicago led Catherine and Eddie to move to Ontario and found the Madonna House. Catherine described Madonna House as "a house of hospitality. It is a place [where] people are received, not according to their education, not according to how wonderful they are as painters or whatever else they can do. They are received simply as people."[10] Catherine met with Pope Pius XII and petitioned for Madonna House to become a secular institute in 1951. Catherine died in 1985, and her cause for canonization was opened in 2000.

Madonna House is still in existence, with active field houses in several continents. They follow the "little mandate" that Catherine believed she received from Jesus. It is essentially a "distillation of the Gospel,"[11] including serving the poor, praying and fasting, and listening to the Holy Spirit.

The Rise of Feminine Entrepreneurship

Taryn

This might sound strange, but one of my favorite things about shopping at small woman-owned businesses is the packaging. Almost without fail, the products I buy from small businesses owned by women come to me beautifully wrapped and, often, with a handwritten "thank you" note and some extra goodies, like a sticker or a bookmark. It's an extra detail that makes me feel valued as a person, not just a wallet.

Similarly, the first time I took my two-year-old to toddler story time at our small-town coffee shop, we were (unusually) the only ones there. Rather than canceling, the owner, who also runs story time, paid extra attention to my daughter. She and I bonded over the fact that we went to the same small women's college in Raleigh. Ever since then, whenever this owner is behind the counter when I'm there with my daughter, she pays just as much attention to my daughter as she does to me, asking her questions and making both of us feel welcome in the type of business where, all too often, small children aren't given much regard.

Are there male business owners who also go out of their way to humanize customer service? Absolutely. However, we believe it's a particular gift of the feminine genius to welcome each customer as a son or daughter of God and treat them accordingly.

Regardless of the industry or type of business (or nonprofit), entrepreneurs have the opportunity to make a difference in the lives of their customers, clients, and partners. There are obvious ways, like ethical sourcing and human resources policies. But, there are also the seemingly small practices that make up how you run your business from day to day—the emails you send your customers, the ways you thank them for their business, and the approach you take when there are customer or employee complaints.

I have never thought of myself as an entrepreneur since I've never technically founded a business. And yet, I've realized recently that I *am* entrepreneurial. I'm really a problem solver. When I see a need, I want to meet it. It's why I decided to become Elise's business partner, and it's why I am constantly coming up with new ideas for products and services, both for CWIB and for possible future organizations. When I couldn't find a daytime Bible study that welcomed children, I created my own. To my knowledge, it's a brand-new "product category."

Research shows that male and female entrepreneurs, on average, have different motivations for starting a business. Women are more likely to start a business in response to an unmet need in their community.[12] Men, on the other hand, are more likely to start a business for "external factors" like having higher status and more influence, having a higher position in a business, and proving that they are successful businessmen. Perhaps this is why the social entrepreneurship sector has more female leaders than other industries.[13]

The COVID-19 pandemic was not great for many people's careers, including women's, as we discussed in the last chapter. However, for some people, it was the spark that ignited their entrance into entrepreneurship. This was especially true for women. In fact, in 2020, the number of businesses started by women was almost equal to the number of businesses started by men—a dramatic change from historic trends.[14] Even by 2022, women were still creating about half of new businesses in the United States.[15] These women are also more likely than their male counterparts to say that their business is doing better than they expected it to.

Why are so many women starting businesses now? They want more flexibility and more control over their schedule and lifestyle, they want to be prepared for financial uncertainty, and they are feeling burned out from the corporate 9–5.[16] Others are retired and view their new season of life as an opportunity to pursue an entrepreneurial dream they'd previously put on hold.[17]

The feminine genius makes a big impact at these businesses. Female owners of small- and medium-sized businesses are more likely to focus on creating a positive work environment, supporting employees' mental health and well-being, and creating opportunities for employees to advance[18]—all of which lead to a happier and more impactful business. As St. John Paul II wrote, "Perhaps more than men, women *acknowledge the person*, because they see persons with their hearts. They see them independently of various ideological or political systems. They see others in their greatness and limitations; they try to go out to them and *help them*" (*Letter to Women*, 12).

Fighting the Mentality of Growth at All Costs

We live in a fast-paced culture. For years, publicly traded companies and startups alike have taken shortcuts and pushed to grow their revenue—at any cost to the customer or the employee. Some entrepreneurs and executives wind up in legal trouble for their unethical practices, such as Sam Bankman-Fried's conviction late in 2023 for fraud and conspiracy. Others seem to be able to get away with taking advantage of their customers; many electronics companies, for example, ensure customers will continue to buy new products by not manufacturing repairable devices. In many cases, they also take advantage of their employees in order to turn a quick profit by paying below living wage in poor working conditions and not providing sufficient breaks and time off.

As Catholic entrepreneurs, we can demonstrate a better path. For instance, at Catholic Women in Business, we've experienced much slower growth than we could have if we didn't make sure our team members had time to focus on supporting and caring for their family. We worked hard to make sure that the cost of our Membership Community adequately conveyed its value without taking advantage of our members. And, we partner with an advertiser only if we believe they have something of value to offer our email subscribers or podcast listeners. These types of practices ensure, as Andreas Widmer says, that our business "exists not to gain profits but to serve people."

A previous employer of mine (Taryn's) was a very small business; at the time that I left the company, I think we only had about twenty employees. We'd seen what felt like fast growth in the six years I'd worked there, but compared to most businesses, it was actually very small. Our president and CEO were focused on making sure that the work we did was valuable to our customers and that the business maintained a positive work environment. Indeed, I loved working at this company and always felt that I was treated fairly and respectfully. We may not have been making tens of millions of dollars, but we were paid and treated well, and we had excellent customer feedback and retention.

Embracing Entrepreneurship

Entrepreneurship is not an exclusive club. It's a path for us to embrace our feminine genius. We must hold our career and our business loosely and remember that they are gifts from our Creator, meant to be cultivated to the best of our ability.

Whether you're the owner of your own business or using entrepreneurial skills as a leader of a team, you can rest assured knowing that when God calls you to entrepreneurship, he will equip you with everything you need.

Questions for Reflection and Discussion

1. If you are an entrepreneur, how can you incorporate the ideas of principled entrepreneurship into your work?
2. If you don't own your own business, how might the ideas in this chapter still apply to your career?

3. Are there any steps you can take as a consumer to advocate for principled entrepreneurship in the companies you purchase from?

EIGHT

WHAT IS AUTHENTIC FEMININE LEADERSHIP?

> Daring leadership is ultimately about serving other people, not ourselves. That's why we choose courage.[1]
>
> Brené Brown in *Dare to Lead*

Taryn

In first grade, I led my own spy ring. I identified troublemakers and told other children to tattle on them. That early and toxic example of leadership aside, I believe in hindsight that I've always been called to leadership but was frequently unsure of what that leadership should look like.

I was elected percussion captain in high school. My role over those two years, and particularly the feeling of pride in the performance of the whole team, not just myself, made me fall in love with leadership. I loved leading practices and helping my teammates grow their skills. The best compliment I've received about my leadership skills to date was after graduation, when the succeeding captain told me that she frequently found herself imitating me.

In college, though, my social anxiety returned in full force. Untreated, it kept me from nurturing my leadership skills—despite being at a small women's college known for developing its students' leadership capabilities. It was a similar story for much of my twenties, and I eventually came to the conclusion that I was not built for leadership.

When I left my last full-time job right before my daughter was born, one of my younger colleagues on the editorial team thanked me for being a mentor to her. I'd never been a manager, yet I'd become a leader.

Now, I co-lead, with Elise, Catholic Women in Business and manage our team of part-time volunteer writers, among other roles. I have served on a nonprofit board of directors and, with my husband, am a leader in our home as a full-time homemaker and mother.

I've realized only recently that I've often conflated leadership and maternity. I thought I was called to work with children, because I always wanted to be a mother. Self-assessments always told me I should work in counseling, because I was other-focused and empathetic. However, I found early in my career that neither teaching nor counseling was the career path I was being called to. Instead, the way I'm called to be a leader outside the home doesn't necessarily have anything to do with children—but it has everything to do with maternity.

I serve my daughter as a physical and spiritual mother, caring for her and helping her to grow and flourish. Spiritual motherhood can—and should—extend outside the home as well, in anything from friendship to business leadership. Ideally, maternity should shape every interaction I have with other people. While I frequently fall short of this goal, I can see motherhood in my empathy, my desire to care for others, and my creativity.

Sometimes, it is easier to see this spiritual motherhood in others—a skill demonstrated by the woman you are about to meet.

Cynthia Psencik: Leading and Mentoring Other Women

Cynthia Psencik is the mentoring program director at the GIVEN Institute, which serves young Catholic women. However, she actually studied fashion merchandising in college and began her career working in the corporate office of a women's apparel retail company.

"There were a lot of shifts in that role," Cynthia told us, and her career ultimately took another direction. "I found myself being led to work in the Archdiocese of New York," she said, "where I went from being a temp administrative assistant in the Hispanic ministry office to my last role there in the Archdiocese as the director of the Office of Youth Ministry." There, her love of people and skills in building relationships blossomed. She was able to combine the communication and administrative skills she learned in her secular jobs with her love of building relationships.

"I realized through my work in the Church that I love people, I love communicating, I love bringing others to the table. And as a leader, I think one of my big skills is, you know, thriving when I see others thriving in their own giftedness," she said. "I also am a natural networker. I know how to . . . bring everyone into a room and help navigate conversations, help navigate dialogue. . . . I almost saw what we say in Spanish, it's called *gente puente*," which directly translates to "person bridge."

"But it's more kind of a bridge builder," Cynthia elaborated. "You know, as someone [who was] born here in the United States from Hispanic parents, I'm also able to navigate the culture seamlessly in both languages. And, as a keen collaborator, which is another skill of mine, invite those who may be missing around the table."

Cynthia says that as women, "we have this tendency to be very affirming of others when we see them, when we see their gifts, and being able to naturally see and allow those opportunities for others to shine."

"I believe that that's one of the gifts I bring as a female leader—my authenticity, my honesty, my compassion, and . . . my strong desire to see in others their giftedness and that they can thrive as beloved daughters and sons of God."

It can be easy to compete with others on where you're going next. Instead, Cynthia said, she considers, "Who am I bringing with me?"

Here, Cynthia shares her tips for finding a mentor:

1. Ask yourself, "Where am I on my journey, and who can I seek to help me get there?" It doesn't have to be job related, and it doesn't have to be someone from work. It could be that you're engaged and wanting to talk with a woman who's been married for a while and goes to your church.
2. Be bold and invite the other woman for coffee.
3. Make it reciprocal. Don't think that just because you aren't as old as the other woman, you don't have anything to offer her.

What Motivates You to Lead?

Elise

I have always been ambitious. I can't remember a day in my life when I didn't have grand dreams. At a young age, those dreams were chasing fame and fortune, but as the Lord has shaped and formed my adulthood, those dreams have become more other-focused: the dream of financially providing for my children to attend college, the dream of helping others reach their full potential, the dream of being able to travel the world.

However, it has seemed that these dreams have always been tied to another part of my heart: anxiety. I have often striven for greatness not out of a desire for holiness but out of a part of me that was formed by trauma and fear. If I could accomplish my dreams, I could stay safe. I could be worthy. I could be loved.

I believe we all have these narratives in our lives. What drives us is a mix of desire for glory and doubt, worry, or a desire to be seen. What does this have to do with leadership? Well in order to be a fruitful leader, you must know your motivations for leadership. Everyone is called to be a leader in some capacity; mothers and fathers lead their families day in and day out. But, if the foundation of your leadership is built on vanity, you will be building your house on sand (Mt 7:26–27).

Leadership is a journey. You're not going to be very good at it when you first start. But, as you venture out, as you become more of the woman he has called you to be, you will become more comfortable. You know the weight of that cloak—its color, its smell, and its frays. You're not afraid to wield it when necessary, but you also know when to lay it down for others.

As I've moved through my career as a leader in entrepreneurship and corporate business, the Lord has purified my ambition. I've continually asked myself, "What does it mean to work from peace and not fear or anxiety?"

This healing has not been linear. I've had to relearn it again and again, especially when transitioning from Ringlet to my family's business. But I know that when I am working in union with the Lord, out of peace and wholeness, my work is ten times more effective.

Authentic feminine leadership includes allowing the Lord to heal your own wounds so that you can be free to do the work you are meant to do and then go out into the world and be a source of healing for others to find their own cloak of leadership. This takes courage and vulnerability, but we have faith in you, and the Lord does as well.

The State of Women in Leadership

Our various leadership roles look different from day to day. Elise leaves the house most days, dressed up and commuting to an office. Taryn works very part time, often from the kitchen table. But, we're both leaders—and we both lead *as women*.

Each year for the past eight years, McKinsey & Co. and LeanIn.org have produced a research report titled *Women in the Workplace*, a summary of their annual study on women in corporate America. Their research has found that not only is the famous glass ceiling still in place, keeping many women out of executive ranks who would otherwise like to be there, but there is also a "broken rung" keeping women from advancing even to their first management position. For every hundred men who are promoted from an entry-level position to a manager role, eighty-seven white women and seventy-three women of color are promoted to a manager role. Women are as ambitious as men—even as we prioritize our families and personal lives.[2]

Despite these discrepancies, female leaders are demonstrating their impact. We are effective leaders with some strengths that are similar to male leaders' and some that are complementary. In fact, organizations that have both men and women on their leadership teams tend to be more successful.[3] Having women in middle management positions improves financial performance, and having women on the senior leadership team improves profitability, social responsibility, and the customer experience.[5] Women can also make the leadership team more risk-aware and more open to change,[6] which can potentially boost innovation.

During the COVID-19 pandemic, female leaders of organizations and governments really shone. As early as June 2020,[7] researchers were commenting that countries led by women seemed to be faring better in terms of number of cases and number of deaths from the coronavirus due to their quick response to the onset of the pandemic. It seems that women were more willing to take economic risks and less likely to take risks in terms of human life than male leaders, possibly due to the way we tend to respond to risk and/or our empathetic, interpersonal approach to leadership. In fact, one analysis of US governor briefings in spring 2020 found that female governors tended to show more empathy *and* more confidence.[8]

There's a phenomenon called the "glass cliff"[9] in which women tend to be promoted into leadership positions during a crisis—putting them on the edge of a cliff, as it were, ready to fail. But, we have strengths as female leaders that actually can make us better leaders when times are challenging. We excel at building relationships, collaborating, inspiring and motivating, and communicating, for example.[10] In addition, women experiencing stress tend to identify small wins and make better decisions than stressed men; they think more calmly and "tend and befriend" the people they are leading, helping to maintain calm throughout the organization.[11] While, previously, research found that women tend to pay a price when they show emotion as leaders, the pandemic may have changed this bias; people wanted to know that their leaders were empathizing with them.[12] During the pandemic, female CEOs demonstrated empathy, adaptability, and accountability in the way they communicated on earnings calls.[13]

Leadership and the Feminine Genius

In his 1988 apostolic letter *Mulieris Dignitatem* (*On the Dignity and Vocation of Woman*), Pope St. John Paul II wrote that "our time in particular *awaits the manifestation* of that 'genius' which belongs to women, and which can ensure sensitivity for human beings in every circumstance: because they are human!—and because 'the greatest of these is love' (cf. 1 Cor 13:13)" (30).

It is this "sensitivity for human beings in every circumstance" that makes us exceptional leaders. We tend to feel more empathy for people who are suffering[14]—as Edith Stein wrote, we "have ears for the softest and most imperceptible little voices."[15] In fact, our brain responds to seeing someone in pain by mimicking what we would feel if we were in the same pain.[16] It is perhaps because of this empathy that we excel at building strong, authentic, and vulnerable relationships; mentoring and developing other people; and being aware of how we can contribute to our community.[17] Women tend to be effective and clear communicators, innovative, supportive, collaborative, and good at inspiring and motivating others,[18] whereas men tend to be more abstract thinkers and risk-takers.[19]

Servant leadership is a particularly feminine approach to leadership. A term first identified by Robert K. Greenleaf in 1970, "servant leadership" is defined as "a philosophy and set of practices that enriches the lives of individuals, builds better organizations and ultimately creates a more just and caring world."[20] Servant leaders are more focused on the people they work with than on their output, and women tend to be gifted servant leaders who also inspire the people who follow them to be servant leaders as well.[21]

As a business owner and consultant, I (Elise) have witnessed a wide range of leadership styles. From beautiful, life-giving encouragement to dictatorship-esque ruling, there are personalities of all different types found in the workplace. One main ingredient I've realized is crucial to virtuous leadership is vulnerability. I know vulnerability is one of my superpowers as a female executive. My team is more likely to trust me if they know me. It requires in-the-moment discernment, but I have seen dramatic shifts in others when I share a story of when I've struggled with a similar issue or express emotion appropriately when in a difficult situation. Vulnerability breaks the barrier that we put up in the workplace, especially in corporate America, where we often feel like we have to have it all together. This vulnerability allows for confidence in one another and strengthens our relationships.

On the other hand, serving others can take its toll; Jesus perfectly embodied the ideal of servant leadership, yet the gospels tell us he frequently left the crowds to pray in solitude. We may be prone, meanwhile, to perfectionism—to striving to appear perfect and to measuring our worth by what we achieve.[22] This perfectionism may cause us to avoid setting boundaries and overlook our own needs. We've certainly both experienced this challenge in our own lives, whether it's being afraid to have a difficult conversation for fear of what someone will think of us or trying to be a perfect mother rather than simply a good one. Without self-awareness, self-care, and confidence, serving can easily turn into people pleasing.

Venerable Mary Lange shows us how true service, lived out according to the will of God, is possible in all circumstances.

Venerable Mary Lange: Seeing God's Work at Hand, Shaping Us

Elizabeth Clarisse Lange was born in the French-speaking part of Cuba to a family of good social standing. She immigrated "with a heart ready for service"[23] to Baltimore, Maryland, where there was a large French-speaking Catholic refugee population due to the Haitian revolution. Despite the fact that she was a Black woman in a state where slavery was legal, she decided to make sure that the children of Caribbean immigrants would receive an education.

In 1829—a time when no US convent would accept a sister of color—Elizabeth started the first religious congregation of Black women, the Oblate Sisters of Providence, taking on the name Sr. Mary. She served as superior general (the first Black American superior general) for the Oblates and established an academy, an orphanage, a widow's home, and a night school for Black adults to learn to read and write. She and her sisters offered spiritual direction and religious education as well as vocational training, and after the Civil War, when Baltimore became a refuge for Black children orphaned in the war, she started caring for them, too.

Under her "pioneering vision and holy example,"[24] the Oblate Sisters of Providence grew quickly, requiring several moves and expansions. Through it all, Mother Lange kept her trust in God's providence. With humility, she served in many capacities, not just as superior general. She even agreed, along with her sisters, to serve as a housekeeper at St. Mary's Seminary in Baltimore.

Mother Mary Lange died in 1882, and the cause for her canonization was opened in 1991. Pope Francis declared her "Venerable" in 2023 in recognition of her "heroic virtue."

"Like each of us," writes Catholic speaker Gloria Purvis, "her life is a mixture of accomplishments and failures. Mother Lange gives us a model for how to see God's hand at work and how we can allow him to shape us." Mother Lange used her own money for service and relied on God, not on herself or other people, for everything. "Time and again in her story," Purvis writes, "we see that if she solely trusted her earthly friends instead of God, she might have crumbled. But she did not crumble—far from it. She persevered, knowing that God is able to do the impossible."[25]

Put Me In, Coach?

Taryn

Coaching hasn't been solely relegated to sports in a long time. Pop culture has made fun of "life coaches" for a while, and senior leaders have been shelling out lots of money to work with executive coaches for a few decades. Now, though, coaching is becoming more popular, more accessible, and more Catholic than ever. We know many Catholic coaches focused on business coaching, leadership development, or mindset coaching—or a combination of these areas. Many of these women focus on coaching other women in business, helping them to become more successful while staying focused on God.

Research I conducted with my former colleague Dr. Amy DuVernet found that providing formal coaching to women improves their leadership development experience.[26] Coaching involves working one-on-one with someone to build skills and identify and work toward goals (career, business, or otherwise). It may be someone you pay on your own, or it may be someone your company pays to work with you as part of a formal leadership development program.

Coaching isn't just something you outsource, though. It's becoming increasingly common for managers to see themselves as coaches for their employees, and coaching is not only a tool for leadership development but a leadership skill, too. In fact, because women tend to be focused on developing their employees, coaching is a natural skill for us to use in conversations with the people we manage. Incorporating coaching skills into our leadership toolbox is a way to humanize the manager-employee relationship and have a more holistic approach to management.

The Mentoring Model

Taryn

As I said earlier, when I left my last job, one of the associate editors thanked me for being a mentor.

I was surprised and touched: I hadn't considered myself a mentor. Sure, I'd answered questions when she had them and taught her how to take over my job before I left. I'd always tried to be encouraging and to model what it meant to be a subject matter expert. But a mentor? I was gratified to know she thought of me that way.

Sometimes, this type of mentoring relationship can be the most effective: the kind that is formed organically, outside of a formal mentoring program. These relationships are more authentic, because they've come about from a natural bond between two people who share interests, career goals, experiences, and even personality traits. If you aspire to leadership, having a mentor in the industry or in a role you want to be in can help you learn what it takes to get there or even if it's what you really want. If you are a leader, whether it's in your job title or, as in my case, otherwise, you're in a great position to be a mentor for someone else. Stay open and get to know other women in your company, industry, or area. You never know what might come of it.

There is a new concept in mentoring that's been sparking conversation in light of today's intergenerational workforce. In reverse mentoring, a younger professional mentors an older professional, and perhaps vice versa. I have this type of relationship with another business owner and mother. Her children are adults now, and she serves as a mentor to me as a new mother. She has more years as a practicing Catholic under her belt by virtue of being older and can be a guide in that way as well. Still, she's told me that she feels we learn from each other—a compliment that I do believe to be true.

We don't have formal conversations where we ask each other set questions or plan goals for meetings. Instead, we typically meet for coffee, my toddler in tow, and just have conversations. We accompany each other, encouraging each other through hard times and asking for advice when we feel the other woman has experience to share.

It's important to note that your mentor doesn't have to be a woman. In fact, if you work in an industry that is heavily male dominated, it may be that a man is the best way for you to learn about becoming a leader in your industry or at your company. We have many examples among the saints of male-female friendships and mentoring relationships. For example, St. Francis de Sales was a great friend and mentor of St. Jane Frances de Chantal, whom you met in chapter 3.

Next, we learn how Valentina Imhoff is building a life of faith around mentoring and helping others find their purpose.

Valentina Imhoff: Helping People Encounter God and Discover Their Purpose

Born in Nigeria to parents she calls adventurous, Valentina Imhoff has also lived in the Cayman Islands, Bermuda, and Nebraska, where she went to college. Valentina's resume includes working in learning and development and leadership training, working in economic development, teaching entrepreneurship in Spanish to high schoolers in Nicaragua, and performing employee engagement analytics at a startup serving Fortune 100 and Fortune 50 companies.

It was in this last role that she realized how many people were unhappy in their jobs or didn't have support to grow their skills and careers. "There's that desire to do well and be successful, but they didn't have the support and direction," she said.

Valentina realized then that what she really wanted was to be able to make an impact on a one-on-one scale rather than at the organizational level. "And I felt God calling me in that direction," she added.

Now, she combines her faith and her learning and development experience in her career coaching business. "The Lord cares about every aspect of our lives," she said. She helps clients with things like their resume or cover letter but also digs deeper, helping them figure out why they're stuck in their career, and brings the Lord into the conversation.

"And honestly," she said, "I love that the most. Like, I want people to find great jobs, but . . . more than anything, I want them to encounter God."

Valentina says that as a female leader, in particular, she brings empathy and encouragement to the proverbial table. She remembers a colleague at a previous job telling her, during a particularly busy and stressful time, "Valentina, your encouragement and your joy is what's keeping me going right now." She believes that process—empathizing with how someone is feeling and then encouraging them—is very important and something she's gifted at.

Valentina has also taken on leadership roles at church, where she's always enjoyed offering spiritual advice and mentorship. In fact, those experiences led Valentina to enroll in an educational program to become a spiritual director. Mentorship, she told us, has "looked different over the years, but I'm thinking back now, it's mostly related to faith, which I get the most excited about anyway."

Virtuous Leadership: A Calling for Everyone

You don't have to have "manager" in your title to be a leader. Whether or not you have formal power, you can influence people and even your organization for the better.[27]

Alexandre Havard, a Catholic leadership expert, believes that "leadership is not reserved to an elite. It is the vocation not of the few but of the many."[28] Virtuous leaders are people—of any title and in any career—who spend their lives striving to grow in virtue. They work to grow their character and become more integrated throughout the course of their lives. And they "are defined by their magnanimity and humility."[29] Magnanimity is the virtue that helps us work toward a great mission. When we combine magnanimity with humility, we become servant leaders.

Elise

I started Catholic Women in Business because I was lonely. I couldn't find another Catholic woman in my community who was also working. My journey in leading Catholic Women in Business started because I took a chance and asked another woman if she felt the same way. I'm grateful that her answer was "Me, too." It sparked a series of conversations that led to the formation of more friendships and made CWIB the welcoming community it is today.

Sometimes, as Catholic women, it's hard to find our place in the Church. As St. John Paul II said, "I plead with you—never, ever give up on hope, never doubt, never tire, and never become discouraged. Be not afraid."[30] Just because something isn't obvious doesn't mean that it isn't true or meant to be. It is in union with Jesus and his Church that you will receive your true calling in life—your mission—and the inspiration and tools to accomplish it all. Jesus is waiting for you in the Eucharist, always. It is there that you will find inspiration and direction.

Leadership and business will require much of you, just like every other facet of your vocation. It will demand resilience and perseverance. It will be a war. But remember, every woman of the Church, every saint who has pursued holiness and her own vocation to business, has set the groundwork for you to walk in your own vocation with confidence. You are never alone.

Now, go forth! Remember that work and leadership are a call to love. "This is my commandment, that you love each other as I have loved you. Greater love has no man than this, that a man lay down his life for his friends" (Jn 15:12–13).

If you follow this commandment of Jesus, you will have all the success you need.

Questions for Reflection and Discussion

1. What do you picture when you picture a leader? What about a female leader?
2. If we are to imitate Jesus in everything (Eph 5:1), how can we change our approach to leadership to be more like him?
3. Would you like to find a mentor? What are three steps you can take in the next week to find one?
4. How can you be a better mentor to other women?
5. What leadership skills do you excel in? How can you nurture those skills in other women?
6. What leadership skills do you need to develop more? Identify three steps you can take in the next week to start cultivating them.

ABOUT CATHOLIC WOMEN IN BUSINESS

Catholic Women in Business is a resource and community for you to grow professionally and spiritually alongside other women.

Whether you're a working mom, a young professional, or a business veteran, fitting work between nap times and kid pickups, or discerning your next steps, we are here to help you integrate your faith and your vocation to business. Our community is full of women from varied professional backgrounds who work full time, part time, or somewhere in between.

Through the free articles on our website by a diverse group of writers, our Facebook group of more than seven thousand women, interviews on the *Catholic Women Lead* podcast with relatable Catholic business women, and our education-based Membership Community, we are here not only to help you navigate your career but also to define what "working" means to you spiritually and personally—so that you can thrive as a Catholic woman in business.

If you're just entering the workforce, we hope to share a vision of what working in business can look like for you. If you're midcareer and seeking meaning and fellowship, we hope our community will inspire you and bring new life to your work and relationships. And, if you've been through it all and would like to give something back, we hope you will share your wisdom and guidance with your fellow Catholic businesswomen in our community.

Wherever you are in your professional career, you are welcome at Catholic Women in Business.

Join us:

- Learn more and read our articles at www.catholicwomeninbusiness.com.
- Listen to our podcast, *Catholic Women Lead*, on Apple Podcasts and Spotify.
- Join our free Facebook group at www.facebook.com/groups/catholicwomeninbusiness.
- Join the CWIB Membership Community at www.catholicwomeninbusiness.com/membership.
- Sign up for our free newsletter at www.catholicwomeninbusiness.com/newsletter.

BIOGRAPHIES OF FEATURED BUSINESSWOMEN

Regina Boyd is a licensed mental health counselor and marriage and family therapist. She is the founder of Boyd Counseling Services, a contributor to the Hallow app, and author of the book *Leaving Loneliness Behind*. Regina has presented extensively on the intersection of mental health and Catholicism for national organizations, and her work has been featured by Catholic Women in Business and FemCatholic and on SiriusXM's The Catholic Channel. She lives with her family in Orlando, Florida, where she assists with parish and diocesan marriage formation. Learn more at www.reginaboyd.com.

Lisa Canning is a mom of ten on earth and one in heaven and is a certified Catholic mindset coach through Metanoia Catholic. Author of *The Possibility Mom: How to Be a Great Mom and Pursue Your Dreams at the Same Time*, Lisa has a passion for coaching Catholic moms in life and business through her online communities, private coaching, and mastermind program. She has been featured on *The Today Show*, *Hallmark Home and Family*, EWTN, the Hallow app, HGTV, and *The New York Times*. Learn more at www.lisacanning.ca.

Delphine Chui is an award-winning journalist, speaker, and charity founder from London. A Catholic revert and former women's magazine editor who experienced "cancel culture" for being publicly pro-life, she is passionate about learning and sharing how to be boldly Catholic in today's world, as well as speaking about God's design for men and women amid modern dating culture on her YouTube channel. Delphine loves to explore themes of intentional living, and, having recently taken the leap to go freelance, she's been reflecting on the definition of "work," embracing ambition at a pace that's conducive to holiness and health. She volunteers as CEO of her canine companionship charity, CareDogs, and has gotten back into writing after a sabbatical to rediscover her voice. You'll most likely find her out in nature walking or multitasking while listening to a podcast. Learn more at www.instagram.com/delphinediscusses.

Leah Darrow is a highly accomplished entrepreneur, mother of seven, and the visionary behind the Motivated Mompreneur program. With her passion for helping others turn their entrepreneurial dreams into reality, Leah has coached numerous business owners and guided hobby entrepreneurs toward becoming successful, full-fledged entrepreneurs, generating income to support both themselves and their families. Learn more at www.leahdarrow.com.

Alexandra Macey Davis is a lawyer, writer, and editor. Currently, she works as the managing editor of *Public Discourse*, an online journal dedicated to renewing the culture through thoughtful reflection on religion, family, and education. Her own writings have appeared in *Catholic Women in Business*, *Verily*, *Plough Quarterly*, *The Federalist*, *FemCatholic*, *Public Discourse*, *Catholic Mom*, *Coffee + Crumbs*, and others, and she also writes on Substack. She lives in Raleigh, North Carolina, with her husband and two young boys. Learn more at www.alexandramaceydavis.substack.com.

Mindy Edgington is a Catholic convert from St. Louis, Missouri. She lives in Nashville, Tennessee, with her husband and their hound dog, Brody. By day, Mindy works as a manager of governance, risk, and compliance for a national behavioral health system. Her hobbies include volunteering, doing laundry, writing, hiking, and reading in her local coffee shops and bars. Learn more at www.instagram.com/mindy.edgington.

Dr. Glory Enyinnaya is a management consultant who worked at Accenture before founding the consulting firm Kleos Advisory. Her research, which focuses on the role of entrepreneurs as change agents, has been published in top-tier publications such as the *Harvard Business Review*. She is a member of the faculty of Pan-Atlantic University in Nigeria. Glory serves as an official of the Legion of Mary in the Archdiocese of Lagos, a cooperator of Opus Dei, and an Associate of the Society of the Holy Child Jesus. Learn more at www.gloryenyinnaya.com.

Valentina Imhoff is a career coach helping women encounter God through their work. She has lived and worked in six countries and has over ten years of experience in a variety of industries. In addition to coaching, she facilitates Called & Gifted workshops to help others discern their charisms. Her greatest loves are her husband, son, and trying new recipes in the kitchen. Learn more at www.fiatcareercoaching.com.

Leah Jacobson, IBCLC, has been working with young people and mothers since 2000. She is a board-certified lactation consultant and founded a nonprofit, the Guiding Star Project, in 2010. In 2021, her first book, *Wholistic Feminism: Healing the Identity Crisis Caused by the Women's Movement,* was published. She joined the University of St. Thomas in Houston, Texas, in 2023 as the program manager for its sexuality and gender studies graduate program. There, she oversees the first-ever master's in Catholic women's and gender studies degree. Leah lives in Minnesota with her husband, Josh, and their seven children. Learn more at www.guidingstarproject.com.

Caroline Kenagy is a young Catholic professional who graduated from the University of Kansas, where she studied marketing and leadership. She has a strong passion for connecting faith and business and has served on the Catholic Women in Business leadership team since 2021.

Caroline currently lives in Chicago and works as an associate marketing manager for Medline Industries, a medical supplies manufacturer. She loves traveling to visit her family and friends and enjoys supporting her favorite sports teams. Learn more at www.linkedin.com/in/carolinekenagy.

Meghan Maloof Berdellans, née Connolly, is a seasoned professional with a background in digital marketing, real estate, and health and wellness. She is dedicated to sharing a healthy lifestyle, emphasizing a return to the roots of our ancestors as well as a mindset that our body is a gift from God, which should be treated as such. She has resided in South Florida since 2016 and works as a Florida real estate broker. Meg sits on numerous boards, including Legatus Miami, the Endometriosis Coalition, Beaux Arts Miami, and Comfort Crusaders, and she is the immediate past president of the Young Professional Philanthropists (YPP) Circle with Miami Women Who Rock. Meg has been married to her husband, Albert Maloof Berdellans III, since June 2019. Learn more at www.megconnolly.com.

Cynthia Psencik is the mentoring program and alumnae director at the GIVEN Institute. She was born and raised in New York City to parents from the Dominican Republic. Cynthia previously served as the vice president of LaRED—National Catholic Network de Pastoral Juvenil Hispana and is a member of the National Federation for Catholic Youth Ministry (NFCYM). She is married to her husband, Evan, and lives in Austin, Texas. Learn more at www.linkedin.com/in/cynthia-psencik-30782716b.

Laura Pugliano is an entrepreneur, wife, and mother of three. She and her husband founded Ciccio's Olives, importing their family's exquisitely pure extra-virgin olive oil along with other artisan products from Southern Italy. Learn more at www.linkedin.com/in/laurapugliano.

Shivonne Sant-Solomon is a wife and mother of two, blessed with the responsibility of raising them in this dynamic world! Over the past nineteen years, Shivonne has had the opportunity to work in a variety of commercial roles within the energy industry as well as assuming the role of a stay-at-home mother to her then-young kids for three years. As Shivonne continues along her spiritual and professional growth and development paths, she seeks out opportunities to share her faith and contribute and support the achievement of the world's energy transition goals in caring for God's creation. Learn more at www.linkedin.com/in/shivonnesantsolomon-sss.

Stacey Sumereau's unique journey spans performing in national Broadway tours of *The Wizard of Oz* and *Beauty and the Beast* to discerning religious life on reality TV in *The Sisterhood: Becoming Nuns*, to marriage and motherhood. She founded and hosted the Be Not Afraid Conference and the God's Adventure Awaits Summit, serving more than twenty thousand people in 2020. Stacey hosts the popular *Called and Caffeinated* podcast and YouTube show. In 2020, she wrote and taught the True North Discernment Course to people in thirteen countries around the world. Stacey has contributed to the Ascension Presents YouTube Channel and has written for the *National Catholic Register*, *Vocations and Prayer Magazine*, and *Life News*. She and her husband, John, are raising their four children (aged six and under) in the Washington, DC, area. She has presented at the National Catholic Youth Conference, the LA Religious Education Congress, and dioceses across the country, encouraging young people to know their worth and to embrace God's adventure. Learn more at www.staceysumereau.com.

Amy Suzanne Upchurch is founder and CEO of Pink Stork, a company owned and operated by women that supports women on their journey to motherhood. But more so, she is a wife and mama to six kids, her motherhood journey filled with obstacles from infertility, severe morning sickness, and a deathbed scare, all with military deployments complicating these challenges. The most recent part of her journey has been navigating raising her youngest, Maximilian, who has Down syndrome. Through this experience, she has learned that we can all make a difference in the world, and she desires to advocate for the Down syndrome community. Learn more at www.pinkstork.com.

FOR FURTHER READING, WATCHING, AND LISTENING

For conversations between Elise and Taryn on the topics in this book, along with other supplemental content, scan the QR code or visit **www.catholicwomeninbusiness.com/holy-ambition**.

Books

- *A Civilization of Love: What Every Catholic Can Do to Transform the World* by Carl Anderson
- *Impact with Wings: Stories to Inspire and Mobilize Women Angel Investors and Entrepreneurs* by Suzanne Andrews, Jagruti Bhikha, and Karen Bairley Kruger
- *Detoured: The Messy, Grace-Filled Journey from Working Professional to Stay-at-Home Mom* by Jen Babakhan
- *Flex Mom: The Secrets of Happy Stay-at-Home Moms* by Sara Blanchard
- *Dare to Lead: Brave Work. Tough Conversations. Whole Hearts* by Brené Brown
- *Living the Feminist Dream: A Faithful Vision for Women in the Church and the World* by Kate Bryan
- *With All Her Mind: A Call to the Intellectual Life*, edited by Rachel Bulman

- *The Possibility Mom: How to Be a Great Mom and Pursue Your Dreams at the Same Time* by Lisa Canning
- *Poustinia: Encountering God in Silence, Solitude and Prayer* by Catherine Doherty
- *You Don't Have to Carry It All: Ditch the Mom Guilt and Find a Better Way Forward* by Paula Faris
- *One Beautiful Dream* by Jennifer Fulwiler
- *Your Blue Flame: Drop the Guilt and Do What Makes You Come Alive* by Jennifer Fulwiler
- *Create Anyway: The Joy of Pursuing Creativity in the Margins of Motherhood* by Ashlee Gadd
- *The Discernment of Spirits: An Ignatian Guide for Everyday Living* by Timothy M. Gallagher, OMV
- *The Myth of the Nice Girl: Achieving a Career You Love without Becoming a Person You Hate* by Fran Hauser
- *Virtuous Leadership: An Agenda for Personal Excellence*, 3rd ed., by Alexandre Havard
- *It's OK to Start with You* and *A Work in Progress: Embracing the Life God Gave You* by Julia Marie Hogan Werner, LCPC
- *How Women Decide: Everyone's Watching You Call the Shots. Here's How to Make the Best Choices* by Therese Huston
- *Carry Strong: An Empowered Approach to Navigating Pregnancy and Work* by Stephanie Kramer
- *A Call to a Deeper Love: The Family Correspondence of the Parents of Saint Thérèse of the Child Jesus, 1863–1885* by Sts. Louis and Zélie Martin
- *The War of Art* by Steven Pressfield
- *Pay Up: The Future of Women and Work (and Why It's Different than You Think)* by Reshma Saujani
- *Ambition Redefined: Why the Corner Office Doesn't Work for Every Woman and What to Do Instead* by Kathryn Sollmann
- *Essays on Woman*, 2nd ed., by Edith Stein
- *The Privilege of Being a Woman* by Alice von Hildebrand
- *The Art of Principled Entrepreneurship: Creating Enduring Value* by Andreas Widmer

Online Resources

- "Pursuing the Reunification of Home and Work" by Erika Bachiochi: https://americancompass.org/pursuing-the-reuinification-of-home-and-work
- "Women Entrepreneurs are Fuelling US Business Growth—Here's How" by Emma Charlton: https://www.weforum.org/agenda/2023/04/women-entrepreneurship-business-growth-jobs
- *The Gospel of Work* video series at the Ciocca Center for Principled Entrepreneurship (Catholic University of America): https://www.cioccacenter.com/the-series
- "Flourishing in Work and Family Life: Considerations for Young Women," summary of a virtual panel (featuring Taryn DeLong) hosted by Alexandra Macey Davis at *The Public Discourse*: https://www.thepublicdiscourse.com/2023/11/91803
- Women's Philanthropy Institute at Indiana University–Purdue University Indianapolis (IUPUI): https://philanthropy.indianapolis.iu.edu/institutes/womens-philanthropy-institute/index.html
- "Righteous Ambition and the Pursuit of Vocation," by Sydney King: https://mackseyjournal.scholasticahq.com/api/v1/articles/27999-righteous-ambition-and-the-pursuit-of-vocation-a-catholic-christian-perspective.pdf
- McKinsey & Co. and LeanIn.org's annual *Women in the Workplace* reports: https://leanin.org/women-in-the-workplace
- St. John Paul II's *Mulieris Dignitatem*: https://www.vatican.va/content/john-paul-ii/en/apost_letters/1988/documents/hf_jp-ii_apl_19880815_mulieris-dignitatem.html
- St. John Paul II's *Laborem Exercens*: https://www.vatican.va/content/john-paul-ii/en/encyclicals/documents/hf_jp-ii_enc_14091981_laborem-exercens.html
- St. John Paul II's *Letter to Artists*: https://www.vatican.va/content/john-paul-ii/en/letters/1999/documents/hf_jp-ii_let_23041999_artists.html
- St. John Paul II's *Letter to Women*: https://www.vatican.va/content/john-paul-ii/en/letters/1995/documents/hf_jp-ii_let_29061995_women.html

Podcasts

- The Anxious Achiever
- Called & Caffeinated
- Catholic Moms Made for Business
- The Catholic Money Show
- Catholic Women Lead (hosted by Taryn and Elise)
- Coffee + Crumbs
- Disrupt Yourself
- Do Something Beautiful
- How'd She Do That?
- The Jen Fulwiler Show
- The Jess Connolly Podcast
- The Kara Goldin Show
- Letters to Women
- Managing Your Fertility
- The Money with Katie Show
- The Possibility Mom
- A Thriving Catholic
- Women at Work from *Harvard Business Review*

NOTES

Introduction: What Is Women's Work?

1. Edith Stein, "The Ethos of Women's Professions," in *Essays on Woman*, trans. Freda Mary Oben, 2nd. ed. (Washington, DC: Institute of Carmelite Studies Publications, 1996), 50–51.

2. Greg Bottaro, "On the Masculine Genius," *Humanum Review* 2, October 11, 2018, www.humanumreview.com/articles/on-the-masculine-genius.

3. Emma Charlton, "Women Entrepreneurs Are Fueling US Business Growth—Here's How," World Economic Forum, April 20, 2023, www.weforum.org/agenda/2023/04/women-entrepreneurship-business-growth-jobs/.

4. Kahlil Gibran, "On Work," *The Prophet* (New York: Knopf, 1923), https://poets.org/poem/work-4.

5. Erika Bachiochi, "Pursuing the Reunification of Home and Work," *American Compass*, July 15, 2022, www.americancompass.org/pursuing-the-reuinification-of-home-and-work/.

6. Stein, "Ethos of Women's Professions," 57.

7. Luke Burgis and Joshua Miller, *Unrepeatable: Cultivating the Unique Calling of Every Person* (Steubenville, OH: Emmaus Road Publishing, 2018), 87.

1. Can Catholic Women Be Ambitious?

1. Rainesford Stauffer, *All the Gold Stars: Reimagining Ambition and the Ways We Strive* (New York: Hachette Book Group, 2023), 226.

2. Sydney King, "Righteous Ambition and the Pursuit of Vocation," *The Macksey Journal* 2, no. 101 (2021), accessed November 25, 2023, www.mackseyjournal.scholasticahq.com/api/v1/articles/27999-righteous-ambition-and-the-pursuit-of-vocation-a-catholic-christian-perspective.pdf.

3. Reese Witherspoon, "We Have to Change the Idea that a Woman with Ambition Is Out Only for Herself," *Glamour*, September 5, 2017, www.glamour.com/story/reese-witherspoon-october-2017-cover-interview.

4. Witherspoon, "We Have to Change the Idea."

5. Alexandre Havard, *Virtuous Leadership: An Agenda for Personal Excellence*, 2nd ed. (Strongsville, OH: Scepter Publishers, Inc., 2007), 4.

6. "Saints," United States Conference of Catholic Bishops, accessed August 30, 2023, www.usccb.org/offices/public-affairs/saints.

7. "Doctors of the Church," *Catholic Answers Encyclopedia*, accessed November 25, 2023, www.catholic.com/encyclopedia/doctors-of-the-church.

8. John Paul II, "Proclamation of St. Thérèse of the Child Jesus and the Holy Face as a 'Doctor of the Church': Homily of Pope John Paul II," Vatican, October 19, 1997, www.vatican.va/content/john-paul-ii/en/homilies/1997/documents/hf_jp-ii_hom_19101997.html.

9. St. Thérèse of Lisieux, *Story of a Soul*, trans. John Clarke, prep. Marc Foley (Washington, DC: Institute of Carmelite Studies Publications, 2019), 328.

10. Letter from Mother Agnès to Father Roulland, quoted in Guy Gaucher, *I Would Like to Travel the World: Thérèse of Lisieux: Miracle-Worker, Doctor, and Missionary*, English ed. (Manchester, NH: Sophia Institute Press, 2023), 19.

11. Rachel Thomas et al., "Women in the Workplace 2021," McKinsey & Co., accessed November 25, 2023, wiw-report.s3.amazonaws.com/Women_in_the_Workplace_2021.pdf.

12. Samantha Masunaga, "Dream of Becoming Your Own Boss? These Women Made It Happen during COVID," *Los Angeles Times*, September 16, 2021, www.latimes.com/business/story/2021-09-16/women-entrepreneurs-covid-pandemic-first-time-business-owners.

13. Kathryn Sollmann, "Women Job Seekers Should Target Small Employers That Can Better Offer Work Flexibility," *Entrepreneur*, October 9, 2018, www.entrepreneur.com/article/320994.

14. "CNBC and Momentive Release Results of 'Women at Work' Annual Survey," *CNBC*, March 1, 2023, www.cnbc.com/2023/03/01/cnbc-and-momentive-release-results-of-women-at-work-annual-survey.html.

15. "Women in the Workplace: 2022," LeanIn.org, accessed November 25, 2023, www.leanin.org/women-in-the-workplace/2022/were-in-the-midst-of-a-great-breakup.

16. Taryn DeLong, "The #BabiesandDreams Trend Women Are Embracing—and Challenging," *FemCatholic*, May 12, 2023, www.femcatholic.com/post/the-babiesanddreams-trend-women-are-embracing-and-challenging.

17. Katherine Morgan Schafler, *The Perfectionist's Guide to Losing Control: A Path to Power and Peace* (New York: Portfolio, 2023), 51.

18. Hephzibah Anderson, "'Girl Boss': When Empowerment Slogans Backfire," *BBC*, January 28, 2020, www.bbc.com/worklife/article/20200127-the-advert-that-triggered-a-debate-about-girl-boss.

19. Amil Niazi, "Losing My Ambition," *The Cut*, March 25, 2022, www.thecut.com/2022/03/post-pandemic-loss-of-ambition.html.

20. Pauline Rose Clance and Suzanne Imes, "The Imposter Phenomenon in High Achieving Women: Dynamics and Therapeutic Intervention," *Psychotherapy Research, Theory, and Practice* 15, no. 3, 1978, www.paulineroseclance.com/pdf/ip_high_achieving_women.pdf.

21. Sheryl Nance-Nash, "Why Imposter Syndrome Hits Women and Women of Color Harder," *BBC*, July 27, 2020, www.bbc.com/worklife/article/20200724-why-imposter-syndrome-hits-women-and-women-of-colour-harder; Ruchika Tulshyan and Jodi-Ann Burey,

"Stop Telling Women They Have Imposter Syndrome," *Harvard Business Review*, February 11, 2021, www.hbr.org/2021/02/stop-telling-women-they-have-imposter-syndrome.

22. "Imposter Syndrome," *Psychology Today*, accessed August 30, 2023, www.psychologytoday.com/us/basics/imposter-syndrome#overcoming-imposter-syndrome.

23. SMART goals are created using objectives that are Specific, Measurable, Achievable, Relevant, and Time-based (SMART). Kimberlee Leonard and Rob Watts, "The Ultimate Guide to S.M.A.R.T. Goals," *Forbes*, May 4, 2022, www.forbes.com/advisor/business/smart-goals/.

24. The term BHAG (Big, Hairy, Audacious Goal) was coined in 1994 in the book *Built to Last: Successful Habits of Visionary Companies* by Jim Collins and Jerry Porras (New York: Harper Business, 1994).

25. "Objectives and Key Results" and "Key Performance Indicators."

26. Fran Hauser, *The Myth of the Nice Girl: Achieving a Career You Love without Becoming a Person You Hate* (New York: Houghton Mifflin Harcourt Publishing Company, 2018), 12.

2. How Do I Discern and Surrender to God's Will for My Career?

1. Therese Huston, *How Women Decide: Everyone's Watching You Call the Shots. Here's How to Make the Best Choices* (Boston: Mariner Books, 2017), 21.

2. Alice von Hildebrand, *The Privilege of Being a Woman* (Ave Maria, FL: Sapientia Press, 2002), 62–63.

3. Kathryn Jean Lopez, "Danielle Bean talks Edith Stein, Catholic womanhood, and Jesus' 'most precious gift,'" *Angelus News*, August 9, 2019, www.angelusnews.com/voices/danielle-bean-talks-edith-stein-catholic-womanhood-and-jesus-most-precious-gift/.

4. Pope Francis, "General Audience," Vatican, August 31, 2022, www.vatican.va/content/francesco/en/audiences/2022/documents/20220831-udienza-generale.html.

5. Huston, *How Women Decide*, 118.

6. "Teresa Benedict [*sic*] of the Cross Edith Stein (1891–1942), nun, Discalced Carmelite, martyr," Vatican, accessed August 30, 2023, www.vatican.va/news_services/liturgy/saints/ns_lit_doc_19981011_edith_stein_en.html.

7. Ken Untener, "Prophets of a Future Not Our Own," United States Conference of Catholic Bishops, accessed August 30, 2023, www.usccb.org/prayer-and-worship/prayers-and-devotions/prayers/prophets-of-a-future-not-our-own.

8. "Charisms," Holy Spirit Catholic Church, accessed August 30, 2023, www.holyspiritfargo.com/charisms.

9. "Charisms FAQ," Catherine of Siena Institute, accessed November 25, 2023, www.files.ecatholic.com/14186/documents/2017/3/Charisms%20Brochure.pdf.

10. This tip comes from the content that email subscribers receive after signing up for Sumereau's email newsletter (available at www.staceysumereau.com).

11. David Scott, *The Love That Made Mother Teresa: How Her Secret Visions and Dark Nights Can Help You Conquer the Slums of Your Heart* (Nashua, NH: Sophia Institute Press, 2016), 41.

12. "St. Mother Teresa of Calcutta," GIVEN, accessed September 1, 2023, www.given-institute.com/st-mother-teresa-of-calcutta.

13. Scott, *The Love That Made Mother Teresa*, 107–108.

14. Brian Kolodiejchuk (ed.), *Mother Teresa, Come Be My Light: The Private Writings of the "Saint of Calcutta"* (New York: Doubleday, 2007).

15. Kolodiejchuk, *Mother Teresa, Come Be My Light*, 336.

16. Edward W. Desmond, "Interview with Mother Teresa: A Pencil in the Hand of God," *Time*, December 4, 1989, www.content.time.com/time/subscriber/article/0,33009,959149,00.html.

17. Elizabeth M. Kelly, *Jesus Approaches: What Contemporary Women Can Learn about Healing, Freedom and Joy from the Women of the New Testament* (Chicago: Loyola Press, 2017), 158.

3. Is It OK to Build Wealth?

1. Kevin Staniewicz, "Sallie Krawcheck: 'More Money in the Hands of Women' Is One of the Best Ways to Improve the Economy," *CNBC*, October 25, 2019, www.cnbc.com/2019/10/25/sallie-krawcheck-more-money-for-women-is-good-way-to-improve-economy.html.

2. "Teresa Benedict of the Cross Edith Stein."

3. Erica Mathews, "Is It OK to Build Wealth as a Catholic?" *Catholic Women in Business*, July 7, 2022, www.catholicwomeninbusiness.com/articles/2022/7/6/is-it-ok-to-build-wealth-as-a-catholic.

4. Louise Perrotta, *Wisdom from the Lives and Letters of St. Francis de Sales and St. Jane Frances de Chantal* (Frederick, MD: The Word Among Us Press, 2000), 15.

5. Laura Kray, Jessica Kennedy, and Margaret Lee, "Now, Women Do Ask: A Call to Update Beliefs about the Gender Pay Gap" (abstract), *Academy of Management Discoveries*, August 15, 2023, www.journals.aom.org/doi/10.5465/amd.2022.0021.

6. Kathryn Valentine and Hannah Riley Bowles, "3 Negotiation Myths Still Harming Women's Careers," *Harvard Business Review*, October 4, 2022, www.hbr.org/2022/10/3-negotiation-myths-still-harming-womens-careers.

7. Sarah Coffey, "Pricing Your Services as a Freelancer," *Catholic Women in Business*, September 3, 2019, www.catholicwomeninbusiness.com/articles/2019/9/3/pricing-your-services-as-a-freelancer.

8. Maria Di Mento, "Lack of Women in Top Roles Hinders Nonprofits, Female Nonprofit Workers Say," *The Chronicle of Philanthropy*, April 28, 2014, www.philanthropy.com/article/lack-of-women-in-top-roles-hinders-nonprofits-female-nonprofit-workers-say.

9. Cynthia Stewart, *The Catholic Church: A Brief Popular History* (Winona, MN: Saint Mary's Press, 2008), www.archive.org/details/catholicchurchbr00phdc/page/322/mode/2up.

10. Ron Pulliam, "Church Giving: Do Women Really Give More Than Men?" Givelify, April 30, 2018, www.givelify.com/blog/church-giving-women-men/.

11. "Gender Matters in Philanthropy," Women's Philanthropy Institute, accessed November 26, 2023, www.philanthropy.iupui.edu/doc/institutes/wpi-gatefold1.pdf.

12. Women's Philanthropy Institute, "Gender Matters in Philanthropy."

13. "How Households Make Giving Decisions," Women's Philanthropy Institute, 2021, www.scholarworks.iupui.edu/server/api/core/bitstreams/717cd2b8-45f9-4133-a3be-f41a2c713329/content.

14. "Giving by and for Women: Understanding High-Net-Worth Donors' Support for Women and Girls," Women's Philanthropy Institute, January 2018, www.scholarworks.iupui.edu/bitstream/handle/1805/15117/giving-by-and-for-women-update180131.pdf.

15. Valeriya Safronova, "How Women Are Changing the Philanthropy Game," *New York Times*, January 30, 2021, www.nytimes.com/2021/01/30/style/mackenzie-scott-priscilla-chan-zuckerberg-melinda-gates-philanthropy.html.

16. Tessa Skidmore et al., "The Women and Girls Index: Measuring Giving to Women's and Girls' Causes," Women's Philanthropy Institute, October 2022, www.scholarworks.iupui.edu/server/api/core/bitstreams/7761a100-7e26-4c8c-b85d-0cfe6862087f/content.

17. Taryn DeLong, "Inside Look: Women Leading the Pro-life Movement," *FemCatholic*, April 20, 2020, www.femcatholic.com/post/facing-goliath-the-women-leading-the-pro-life-movement.

18. "Giving Circle Membership: How Collective Giving Impacts Donors," Women's Philanthropy Institute, 2018, www.scholarworks.iupui.edu/server/api/core/bitstreams/0d9ee206-2d87-4fd2-81b1-b48f41c8a811/content.

19. Katie Gatti Tassin, "Shifting Your Money Mindset from Scarcity to Abundance," *Money with Katie*, December 7, 2020, www.moneywithkatie.com/blog/shifting-your-money-mindset-from-scarcity-to-abundance.

4. How Do I Build Strong Relationships at Work?

1. Hauser, *Myth of the Nice Girl*, xi.

2. Edith Stein, "Fundamental Principles of Women's Education," in *Essays on Woman*, trans. Freda Mary Oben (Washington, DC: ICS Publications, 1996), 132.

3. Tomas Chamorro-Premuzic and Cindy Gallop, "7 Leadership Lessons Men Can Learn from Women," *Harvard Business Review*, April 1, 2020, www.hbr.org/2020/04/7-leadership-lessons-men-can-learn-from-women; "New Research Shows Women Are Better at Using Soft Skills Crucial for Effective Leadership and Superior Business Performance, Finds Korn Ferry," Korn Ferry, March 7, 2016, www.kornferry.com/about-us//press/new-research-shows-women-are-better-at-using-soft-skills-crucial-for-effective-leadership.

4. John Kirvan (ed.), *Teresa of Ávila: Let Nothing Disturb You* (South Bend, IN: Ave Maria Press, 2008), 56.

5. Jim Collins, "Level Five Leadership," accessed December 5, 2023, www.jimcollins.com/concepts/level-five-leadership.html.

6. Ryne A. Sherman, "Humility, Leadership and Organizational Effectiveness," *Training Industry*, May 1, 2018, www.trainingindustry.com/articles/leadership/humility-leadership-and-organizational-effectiveness/.

7. Jen Christensen, "All around the World, Women Are Better Empathizers than Men, Study Finds," *CNN*, December 27, 2022, www.cnn.com/2022/12/26/health/empathy-women-men/index.html; David Olmos, "When Watching Others in Pain, Women's Brains

Show More Empathy," UCLA Newsroom, February 27, 2019, www.newsroom.ucla.edu/stories/womens-brains-show-more-empathy.

8. Carl R. Rogers and Richard E. Farson, "Active Listening," in *Communicating in Business Today*, ed. Ruth G. Newman, Marie A. Danziger, and Mark Cohen (Lexington, MA: D.C. Heath & Company, 1987), www.wholebeinginstitute.com/wp-content/uploads/Rogers_Farson_Active-Listening.pdf.

9. Heather R. Younger, *The Art of Active Listening: How People at Work Feel Heard, Valued, and Understood* (Oakland, CA: Berrett-Koehler Publishers, 2023).

10. Edith Stein, *Essays on Woman*, 2nd ed., trans. Freda Mary Oben (Washington, DC: Institute of Carmelite Studies Publications, 1996), 78.

11. Vivek Murthy, "Work and the Loneliness Epidemic," *Harvard Business Review*, September 26, 2017, www.hbr.org/2017/09/work-and-the-loneliness-epidemic.

12. Richard Weissbourd, Milena Batanova, Virginia Lovison, and Eric Torres, "Loneliness in America: How the Pandemic Has Deepened an Epidemic of Loneliness and What We Can Do About It," Harvard Graduate School of Education Making Caring Common Project, February 2021, www.static1.squarespace.com/static/5b7c56e255b02c683659fe43/t/6021776bdd04957c4557c212/1612805995893/Loneliness+in+America+2021_02_08_FINAL.pdf.

13. Daniel L Surkalim et al., "The Prevalence of Loneliness across 113 Countries: Systematic Review and Meta-Analysis," *BMJ*, 2022, www.bmj.com/content/376/bmj-2021-067068.

14. "New Surgeon General Advisory Raises Alarm about the Devastating Impact of the Epidemic of Loneliness and Isolation in the United States," US Department of Health and Human Services, May 3, 2023, www.hhs.gov/about/news/2023/05/03/new-surgeon-general-advisory-raises-alarm-about-devastating-impact-epidemic-loneliness-isolation-united-states.html.

15. Taryn Oesch and Amy DuVernet, "Developing Women Leaders in Business: Research Insights and Best Practices," in *Global Perspectives on Women's Leadership and Gender (In)Equality*, ed. Elena V. Shabliy, Dmitry Kurochkin, and Gloria Y. A. Ayee (Cham, Switzerland: Palgrave Macmillan, 2020), 117–63.

5. How Do I Keep the Faith in a Secular Workplace?

1. "Doctor," Society of Saint Gianna, accessed November 26, 2023, www.saintgianna.org/doctor.htm.

2. Tadeusz Pacholczyk, "Medical Circumstances of St. Gianna," Society of Saint Gianna, accessed November 26, 2023, www.saintgianna.org/medicalcircum.htm.

3. Pacholczyk, "Medical Circumstances of St. Gianna."

4. Pacholczyk, "Medical Circumstances of St. Gianna."

5. Ignatius of Loyola, *The Autobiography of St. Ignatius of Loyola*, trans. Joseph F. Callaghan, ed. Jon C. Olin (New York: Fordham University Press, 1993).

6. How Do I Juggle Faith, Work, and Family?

1. Stephanie Kramer, *Carry Strong: An Empowered Approach to Navigating Pregnancy and Work* (New York: Penguin Books, 2023), 155.

2. Kramer, *Carry Strong*, xxvi.

3. Alisha Haridasani Gupta, "Why Some Women Call This Recession a 'Shecession,'" *New York Times*, May 9, 2020, www.nytimes.com/2020/05/09/us/unemployment-coronavirus-women.html.

4. Stefania Fabrizio, Diego B. P. Gomes, and Marina M. Tavares, "COVID-19 She-Cession: The Employment Penalty of Taking Care of Young Children," International Monetary Fund, March 2021, www.imf.org/-/media/Files/Publications/WP/2021/English/wpiea2021058-print-pdf.ashx.

5. Taryn Oesch, "A New 'Mommy Track': How Returnships Can Help Close the Gender Gap," *Training Industry*, March 30, 2018, www.trainingindustry.com/articles/diversity-equity-and-inclusion/a-new-mommy-track-how-returnships-can-help-close-the-gender-gap/.

6. Mark-Mary Ames, "An Easy Way to Do a Daily Examen," Ascension Presents, January 11, 2019, video, www.youtube.com/watch?v=FUcoHAqOFRs&t=33s.

7. Catherine Doherty, *Poustinia: Encountering God in Silence, Solitude and Prayer* (Combermere, ON: Madonna House Classics, 2000), 11.

8. Nikki Nash, "Building an Empire Like a Mother w/ Julie Cole," September 22, 2023, in *The Market Your Genius Podcast*, podcast, www.podcasts.apple.com/us/podcast/building-an-empire-like-a-mother-w-julie-cole-ep-257/id1461675387?i=1000628804597.

9. Benedict XVI, "Address to the German Pilgrims Who Had Come for the Inauguration Ceremony of the Pontificate," Vatican, April 25, 2005, www.vatican.va/content/benedict-xvi/en/speeches/2005/april/documents/hf_ben-xvi_spe_20050425_german-pilgrims.html.

10. Leah Darrow, *The Other Side of Beauty: Embracing God's Vision for Love and True Worth* (Nashville: Thomas Nelson, 2017).

7. How Can I Make a Difference as a Catholic Entrepreneur?

1. Emily Landers, "Mimi Striplin, Founder of The Tiny Tassel, Reflects on Perseverance, Creativity, and How She Is Building a Brand That Is Breaking Down Barriers," October 3, 2023, in *How'd She Do That*, podcast, www.podcasts.apple.com/us/podcast/170-mimi-striplin-founder-of-the-tiny-tassel-reflects/id1511420962?i=1000630030554.

2. Andreas Widmer is now the founder and director of the Ciocca Center for Principled Entrepreneurship at the Catholic University of America's Busch School of Business.

3. Andreas Widmer, *The Art of Principled Entrepreneurship: Creating Enduring Value* (Dallas: Matt Holt Books, 2022), 39.

4. Widmer, *The Art of Principled Entrepreneurship*, 63.

5. Widmer, *The Art of Principled Entrepreneurship*, 108.

6. Widmer, *The Art of Principled Entrepreneurship*, 102.

7. Widmer, *The Art of Principled Entrepreneurship*, 130.

8. Widmer, *The Art of Principled Entrepreneurship*, 148.

9. Widmer, *The Art of Principled Entrepreneurship*, 69.

10. David Meconi (ed.), *Catherine de Hueck Doherty: Essential Writings* (Maryknoll, NY: Orbis Books, 2009), 34.

11. "The Little Mandate," Madonna House Apostolate, accessed November 26, 2023, www.madonnahouse.org/about/the-little-mandate/.

12. Natanya Meyer, Chris Schachtebeck, and Cecile Nieuwenhuizen, "Motivation and Intention of Small Business Entrepreneurs: A Gender Perspective," *Journal of Small Business Strategy* 32, no. 4 (2022), www.jsbs.scholasticahq.com/api/v1/articles/40316-motivation-and-intention-of-small-business-entrepreneurs-a-gender-perspective.pdf.

13. Niels Bosma, Thomas Schøtt, Siri Terjesen, and Penny Kew, "Global Entrepreneurship Monitor 2015 to 2016: Special Report on Social Entrepreneurship," Global Entrepreneurship Research Association, 2016, www.gemconsortium.org/file/open?fileId=49542.

14. Anne Stych, "Will This Boom Be Different?" *Bizwomen*, October 5, 2023, www.bizjournals.com/bizwomen/news/profiles-strategies/2023/10/women-small-business-week-main-bar.html?page=all.

15. Alex Tanzi, "Women Are Still the Driving Force of US Post-Covid Entrepreneurs," *Washington Post*, March 30, 2023, www.washingtonpost.com/business/on-small-business/2023/03/30/women-are-still-the-driving-force-of-us-post-covid-entrepreneurs/aa356ebc-cee6-11ed-8907-156f0390d081_story.html.

16. Tanzi, "Women Are Still the Driving Force of US Post-Covid Entrepreneurs."

17. Joseph Coughlin, "Men View Retirement as a Final Chapter while Many Women See a Fresh Start," *Forbes*, April 5, 2023, www.forbes.com/sites/josephcoughlin/2023/04/05/men-view-retirement-as-a-final-chapter-while-many-women-see-a-fresh-start/.

18. "Women Small Business Owners Take Fewer Risks, Have Investment Confidence Gaps," *HerMoney*, October 26, 2023, www.hermoney.com/earn/entrepreneurship/women-small-business-owners-take-fewer-risks-have-investment-confidence-gaps/.

8. What Is Authentic Feminine Leadership?

1. Brené Brown, *Dare to Lead: Brave Work. Tough Conversations. Whole Hearts* (New York: Penguin Random House, 2018), 69.

2. Rachel Thomas et al., "Women in the Workplace 2023," McKinsey & Co., accessed November 26, 2023, www.mckinsey.com/~/media/mckinsey/featured%20insights/diversity%20and%20inclusion/women%20in%20the%20workplace%202023%20v2/women-in-the-workplace-2023-full-report.pdf?shouldIndex=false.

3. Oesch and DuVernet, "Developing Women Leaders in Business," 117–63.

4. Katy Marquardt Hill, "Why and When Gender Diversity in Middle Management Gives Companies a Competitive Advantage," *CU Boulder Today*, July 18, 2023, www.colorado.edu/today/2023/07/18/why-and-when-gender-diversity-middle-management-gives-companies-competitive-advantage.

5. Corinne Post, Boris Lokshin, and Christophe Boone, "Research: Adding Women to the C-Suite Changes How Companies Think," *Harvard Business Review*, April 6, 2021, www.hbr.org/2021/04/research-adding-women-to-the-c-suite-changes-how-companies-think.

6. Post, Lokshin, and Boone, "Research."

7. Supriya Garikipati and Uma Kambhampati, "Leading the Fight against the Pandemic: Does Gender 'Really' Matter?" Social Science Research Network, January 12, 2021, www.papers.ssrn.com/sol3/papers.cfm?abstract_id=3617953.

8. Kayla Sergent and Alexander D. Stajkovic, "Women's Leadership Is Associated with Fewer Deaths during the COVID-19 Crisis: Quantitative and Qualitative Analyses of United States Governors," *Journal of Applied Psychology* 105, no. 8 (2020), www.psycnet.apa.org/fulltext/2020-47004-001.html.

9. Michelle K. Ryan and S. Alexander Haslam, "The Glass Cliff: Evidence that Women Are Over-Represented in Precarious Leadership Positions," *British Journal of Management* 16 (2005), www.is.muni.cz/el/1423/jaro2017/VPL457/um/62145647/Ryan_Haslam_The_Glass_cliff.pdf.

10. Jack Zenger and Joseph Folkman, "Research: Women Are Better Leaders during a Crisis," *Harvard Business Review*, December 30, 2020, www.hbr.org/2020/12/research-women-are-better-leaders-during-a-crisis.

11. Susan R. Vroman and Tiffany Danko, "Against What Model? Evaluating Women as Leaders in the Pandemic Era," *Gender, Work & Organization*, 2020, 1–8, www.doi.org/10.1111/gwao.12488.

12. Vroman and Danko, "Against What Model?"

13. Daniela Brandazza et al., "Leadership in Turbulent Times: Women CEOs during COVID-19," *S&P Global*, May 25, 2021, www.spglobal.com/en/research-insights/featured/special-editorial/women-ceos-covid.

14. Joshua Alvarado, "Women More Likely than Men to Report Feeling Empathy for Those Suffering," Pew Research Center, January 28, 2022, www.pewresearch.org/short-reads/2022/01/28/in-u-s-women-more-likely-than-men-to-report-feeling-empathy-for-those-suffering/.

15. Edith Stein, "Principles of Women's Education," 134.

16. Olmos, "When Watching Others in Pain."

17. Cynthia Adams and Lani Van Dusen, "Understanding the Differences in Reactive and Creative Orientations between Female and Male Leaders," Leadership Circle, March 2022, www.leadershipcircle.com/wp-content/uploads/2022/03/Research-on-Female-and-Male-Leaders-White-Paper-2022-03-17.pdf.

18. Oesch and DuVernet, "Developing Women Leaders in Business," 117–63.

19. "Why Organisations [sic] Should Hire More Women Leaders," Lumina Learning, accessed September 1, 2023, www.luminalearning.com/women-leaders/.

20. "What Is Servant Leadership?" Robert K. Greenleaf Center for Servant Leadership, 2021, www.greenleaf.org/what-is-servant-leadership/.

21. Matthew Biddle, "Women Have the Advantage in Servant Leadership," *UB Now*, January 7, 2020, www.buffalo.edu/ubnow/stories/2020/01/lemoine-servant-leadership.html.

22. Adams and Van Dusen, "Understanding the Differences."

23. Michael R. Heinlein, *Black Catholics on the Road to Sainthood* (Huntington, IN: Our Sunday Visitor Publishing Division, 2021), 67.

24. Heinlein, *Black Catholics on the Road to Sainthood*, 69.

25. Gloria Purvis, “Lange: A School of Confidence in Providence,” in *Black Catholics on the Road to Sainthood*, ed. Michael R. Heinlein (Huntington, IN: Our Sunday Visitor Publishing Division, 2021), 73–78.

26. Oesch and DuVernet, “Developing Women Leaders in Business,” 117–63.

27. Taryn DeLong, “‘For a Time Like This: Informal Leadership and Queen Esther,” *Catholic Women in Business*, July 3, 2023, www.catholicwomeninbusiness.com/articles/2023/7/3/for-a-time-like-this-informal-leadership-and-queen-esther.

28. Havard, *Virtuous Leadership*, xiii.

29. Havard, *Virtuous Leadership*, xvii.

30. Attributed to St. John Paul II.

Taryn DeLong is the copresident and editor-in-chief of Catholic Women in Business. She is a freelance writer and editor for publications such as the Public Discourse, CatholicMom.com, Natural Womanhood, Radiant magazine, Well-Read Mom, and FemCatholic. She is also cohost of the *Catholic Women Lead* podcast.

DeLong earned a bachelor of arts degree in psychology from Meredith College and has been an assistant editor at FemCatholic.

She lives in North Carolina with her family.

everydayroses.blog
Facebook: @everydayroses
Instagram: @tarynmdelong
Substack: everydayroses.substack.com

Elise Crawford Gallagher is copresident and founder of Catholic Women in Business and the chief operations officer at JC Law, a regional law firm based in Baltimore, MD.

Gallagher holds a master of arts degree in communications from Johns Hopkins University and is a 2020 graduate of Goldman Sachs' 10,000 Small Businesses program. Gallagher was the founder and CEO of RINGLET, a marketing agency focused on serving women-owned businesses. She is a life and business coach, speaker, and serial entrepreneur.

She lives with her family in the DC–Baltimore area.

Instagram: @elisecrawfordgallagher

Michelle Hillaert is the executive director of the GIVEN Institute.